TRAINING FOR THE COMPLETE ROWER

A GUIDE TO IMPROVING PERFORMANCE

TRAINING FOR THE COMPLETE ROWER

A GUIDE TO IMPROVING PERFORMANCE

Paul Thompson and Alex Wolf

THE CROWOOD PRESS

First published in 2016 by
The Crowood Press Ltd
Ramsbury, Marlborough
Wiltshire SN8 2HR

www.crowood.com

This impression 2017

© Paul Thompson and Alex Wolf 2016

All rights reserved. No part of this publication may be reproduced or transmitted in any form or by any means, electronic or mechanical, including photocopy, recording, or any information storage and retrieval system, without permission in writing from the publishers.

British Library Cataloguing-in-Publication Data
A catalogue record for this book is available from the British Library.

ISBN 978 1 78500 086 7

Acknowledgements
Alex and Paul would like to thank the following people who helped with the putting together of this book. Katie Mountain has been more help than she could have ever imagined; Katie, we hope you have picked a few tips. Thanks to Dr Mark Homer, Nicole Chase, Katie James, Mike Naylor and Jamie Thomas for their contributions and to Heather Stanning, Helen Glover, Katherine Grainger, Vicky Thornley, Chris Bartley, Rob Morgan, Chris Boddy, Jamie Cheeseman, Matthew Thompson and Zak Lee-Green for being such fine models. Thank you to Sam Scrimgeour and Richard Chambers for being such good cyclists and to well-respected sports photographer Peter Spurrier of Intersport Images for the cover photos of Katherine and Anna. And finally, thank you too to 2012 Olympic double sculls champions Anna Watkins and Katherine Grainger for their foreword to this book, and to Professor Alison McGregor for her advice to both authors.

Dedication
To the athletes we coach – without them this book wouldn't have come about.

Disclaimer
Please note that the authors and publisher of this book do not accept any responsibility whatsoever for any error or omission, nor any loss, injury, damage, adverse outcome or liability suffered as a result of the use of the information contained in this book, or reliance upon it. Since some of the training exercises can be dangerous and could involve physical activities that are too strenuous for some individuals to engage in safely, it is essential that a doctor be consulted before training is undertaken.

Throughout the book 'he', 'him' and 'his' are used as neutral pronouns and as such refer to both males and females.

Typeset by Servis Filmsetting Ltd, Stockport, Cheshire
Printed and bound in India by Parksons Graphics

CONTENTS

	Foreword	6
	Preface	7
	Introduction	8
1	Performance, Training and Physiological Principles	9
2	Training and Technique	19
3	Rowing Training	38
4	Ergometer Training	46
5	Specific Rowing Conditioning	52
6	Strength Training	56
7	Monitoring and Assessing Land Training	76
8	Mobility and Flexibility	81
9	Weightlifting Technique	91
10	Trunk	104
11	Nutrition	114
12	Mental Skills	121
13	Conclusion	125
	Index	126

FOREWORD

Anyone who loves sport will remember moments of pure magic. Moments where the drama of the occasion combines with powerful emotion, where inspiration and excellence meet and where the impossible becomes a reality. For athletes, coaches and the multitude of experts who work behind the scenes in sport those moments make the hard work, the sleepless nights, the stress, the disappointments and the exhaustion all worthwhile. They are indeed magical moments, but the illusion of mystery or surprise invariably belies years of planning, strategy, experience and expertise. The seeds have always been planted long before.

Our rowing careers started out just for fun, but over time our ambitions grew and after a while we joined the British Rowing Team, when rowing at the Olympics became a serious target. It was within the National Team that we began working with Paul Thompson as Chief Coach; he has masterminded the success of the women's and lightweight rowing squads in Great Britain for the past three Olympic Games. Alex Wolf joined the rowing team as our strength and conditioning expert at the beginning of the London Olympiad and we worked closely with him for the following four years. Paul and Alex planned a programme with one goal in mind: to win gold at our home Olympics in London.

One of the keys to that success was diligently focusing on the details of performance and making use of every possible gain in every possible area. Alex and Paul's innovation enabled us to break new ground, expanding our abilities, knowledge and skills. This sense of limitless learning is one of the wonderful things expert coaching helps bring to our sport; there are always new and challenging ways to train. Our team pushed the frontiers in areas as diverse as nutrition, psychology, physiology and strength and conditioning, as well as technical and physical improvements on the water and the ergo. We were lucky enough to be working with the best in the business; it was the leadership of Paul together with the expertise of Alex that drove our development as we prepared for London 2012.

Whatever your level, this book can help you to make progress. For an elite athlete the Olympics is the pinnacle of performance, but throughout our journeys the incremental steps have always been similar. We have always sought the next level of fitness, technical improvement and strength gain. Alex and Paul share a passion for sport and performance and a hunger to continuously seek better, smarter, more effective and more efficient ways of achieving this. With the approaches detailed in this book, we were able to break records on the water and on the rowing machine and face our Olympic final feeling totally prepared and genuinely excited about the challenge. Regardless of your starting point, the guidance in this book will help you take the next steps towards your own goal and to making your own magic. Good luck!

Katherine and Anna
Dr Katherine Grainger CBE and
Anna Watkins MBE

PREFACE

We started working together in 2009 and over the years developed a close working relationship and became friends. Many a long hour we would be discussing training and athletic performance, new research, training techniques and exploring opportunities for gains with the athletes we were working with. We were both privileged to be working with a talented group of athletes, coaches and support staff up to the 2012 Olympic Games, where the British team topped the medal table in stunning style. When the opportunity came for us to consider writing a book we saw it as a good challenge for us to share our thoughts and views on training for rowing and help people who want to improve and progress from where they are. We hope you will see the principles and rationale behind what we say, enabling you to challenge your thinking and challenge us but most importantly to be able to train and perform better today than you did yesterday.

Paul and Alex

Co-author Paul Thompson with Olympic Gold Medallists Anna Watkins and Katherine Grainger.

INTRODUCTION

Rowing is a fantastic sport. It is open to all ages and there is a large selection of ways to enjoy it and also compete in it. Rowers can be found on the rivers, lakes, canals and oceans of the world. They can also be found sweating on indoor rowing machines in boat houses, gyms and homes.

There are many reasons why people row: the feel of the boat gliding through the water; the strength of rhythm and teamwork in a crew; the satisfaction of shared victory in a tight race; the pain, relief and gratification of getting a personal best on the rowing ergometer; or the constant desire to improve and win World Championship and Olympic titles.

This book aims to provide and challenge coaches and rowers with best practice, advice, principles and training programmes to improve their rowing experience and performance. Regardless of whether you are looking to improve on-water performance, an indoor rowing personal best or the quality of your training, you will find something of value in the chapters ahead.

Teamwork and the sense of rhythm are just two reasons why competitive rowing is such a popular sport.

CHAPTER 1

PERFORMANCE, TRAINING AND PHYSIOLOGICAL PRINCIPLES

> **KEY COMPONENTS OF A 2,000M RACE**
>
> 2,000m rowing races are mentally demanding and physically challenging. Competition is fierce and most races are won or lost in the training and preparation the rower or crew does on a day-to-day basis before the event.
>
> The long winter miles outdoors in all weather, lifting weights, working on technique or gruelling ergometer sessions are all part of a rower's tapestry of preparation that will come together over 240 strokes rowed completely in unison with his crewmates.
>
> Rowing involves strength, endurance, rhythm and technique. The longer the strokes, the more power can be applied effectively and efficiently, producing and maintaining a faster boat speed.
>
> Race pacing has to have been developed through training, along with the mental toughness to push on, stay in time and rhythm while delivering power when the rower is in oxygen debt.
>
> Training and its intent needs to reflect these elements and allow the rower to develop, improve and thrive in a competitive environment.
>
> **Key performance contributors in a 2,000m race:**
> Stroke length   Rate
> Power   Effectiveness
> Rhythm   Efficiency

The first step in planning for a performance is to understand and define the event and work out what will be required to achieve your aspiration. What training modalities will be required to support it? How much training volume will be needed and at what intensities? How do you mix the training volume and intensity? Rowers, are you supple enough to get into the rowing length and position to maximize your potential? Are you strong enough to hold that form? Do you have enough conditioning to hold that form under training and performance load and duress?

A 2,000m rowing performance on the ergometer or water is predominantly a high level aerobic activity, using energy derived from the body's uptake of oxygen for approximately 75–85 per cent of its duration, with the remaining 15–25 per cent of effort coming from the body's anaerobic capacities (energy sources that do not rely on oxygen uptake). As a rule of thumb, this percentage breakdown is a good guide for the split of anaerobic and aerobic training that should be done by a rower.

The figure below shows a 2,000m ergometer performance profile. Knowing a rower's oxygen consumption (VO_2) at a given workload (watts) allows the calculation of his

Performance, Training and Physiological Principles

Fig. 1.1: Aerobic and anaerobic contribution of a 2,000m ergometer performance.

oxygen demand and delivery. The wattage gap between oxygen supply and demand shows the anaerobic contribution to the performance.

Energy systems

The body gains energy to function from the food that it ingests. Food is stored as glycogen and fat. Glycogen and fat are broken down by oxygen to form adenosine triphosphate (ATP). ATP is the 'engine room' energy-carrying molecule of the muscles' cells. When a muscle contracts it is the process of ATP converting to energy that allows the muscle to contract.

Protein is also used as an energy source for the body and is integral to muscle growth. Protein consists of the body's building blocks: amino acids. There are eight amino acids that are essential to life, as they cannot be generated by the body alone. Protein post-exercise is important for muscle repair and recuperation as well as optimizing glycogen storage.

The body is able to convert these fuel stores into energy at very different rates. The quickest is the **alactic system,** which predominately utilizes creatine phosphate to produce very explosive short-duration energy for up to approximately 10 seconds (ATP-CP system).

When exercise is at a low and moderate level the heart and lungs have enough capacity to supply the muscles with oxygen, break down glycogen/glucose and fats and remove the waste products of water and carbon dioxide to produce a sustainable extended energy system. As oxygen is the driver, this process is known as the **aerobic pathway**.

As the intensity of physical effort rises, or when the demand for energy changes quickly, the aerobic metabolism can no longer keep pace with the breakdown of stored fuels. In this state the body is producing energy in an **anaerobic pathway**, i.e. without oxygen. A by-product of this process is lactate, which is recycled by muscles with spare aerobic capacity or by the liver. When the lactate production is greater than that which can be recycled, lactate accumulation occurs in the muscle cell and results in metabolic acidosis, which is associated with both muscle pain and fatigue. As the body still requires oxygen to break down the acidosis, it goes into oxygen debt, from which it can recover only after exercise has finished. People feel this as breathlessness after strenuous exercise.

All three of these systems play a part in meeting the metabolic needs of a 2,000m race.

Training can develop the capacity and efficiency of the respiratory, circulatory and muscular systems that deliver energy in the aerobic system. Nutrition and session sequencing can also provide efficiency and optimize fuelling to achieve training adaptation.

Performance, Training and Physiological Principles

Fig. 1.2: Energy systems involved in a 2,000m race.

Respiratory system
When breathing, the body drags oxygen into the respiratory system from the air through the nose and mouth and into the lungs, where the oxygen passes into the bloodstream through the alveoli and on to the circulatory system. The oxygen binds with red blood cells and passes through a series of systems in the body. Oxygen, bound to the red blood cells, flows through the larger arteries down to the smallest arteries, the capillaries. The capillaries encompass the muscle fibres and provide the environment for the chemical exchange between the blood and the muscle cell. Oxygen diffuses from the blood to the muscle cell mitochondria where it is used in the conversion from fuel to energy.

As rowing is an activity that is predominantly aerobic, these systems offer the greatest training performance gains.

Training of the respiratory system can be done with commercially available breathing devices, which help to train and strengthen the breathing muscles in the diaphragm.

Circulatory system
Long-distance endurance training improves the efficiency of the capillarization process, allowing the delivery of more oxygen to the muscle cell and also improving the removal of waste products like lactic acid.

Aerobic training also has a positive training adaptation to the cardiac output of the heart, improving the rate of blood flow and volume of red blood cells going to the muscle fibres. This higher-end aerobic training provides increased capacity and more efficient oxygen delivery to the muscle cells.

Muscularity
Training a rower's muscularity is an important area to address. Muscle fibres play a vital role. There are primarily two types of muscle fibres: fast and slow twitch fibres. Fast twitch are either fast high-oxidative or glycolytic fibres that produce greater power than slow twitch fibres but also fatigue more quickly. Slow twitch fibres are slow-oxidative fibres that are aerobic, so are slow to fatigue and can provide a

Performance, Training and Physiological Principles

lot of muscle energy over a long time. Muscles have multiple fibres in them, but it is possible to train these fibres to increase strength and endurance.

The secret in a training programme is stimulating, loading and maximizing the adaptation to these energy systems. The key to its delivery is monitoring the rower's training so that he can have consistency in his training adherence.

Anaerobic and aerobic balance in a 2,000m performance

There is a strong correlation between 2,000m rowing or ergometer performance and the maximum rate a rower can take up and use oxygen from the air. This is known to sport scientists and coaches as a rower's VO2 Max.

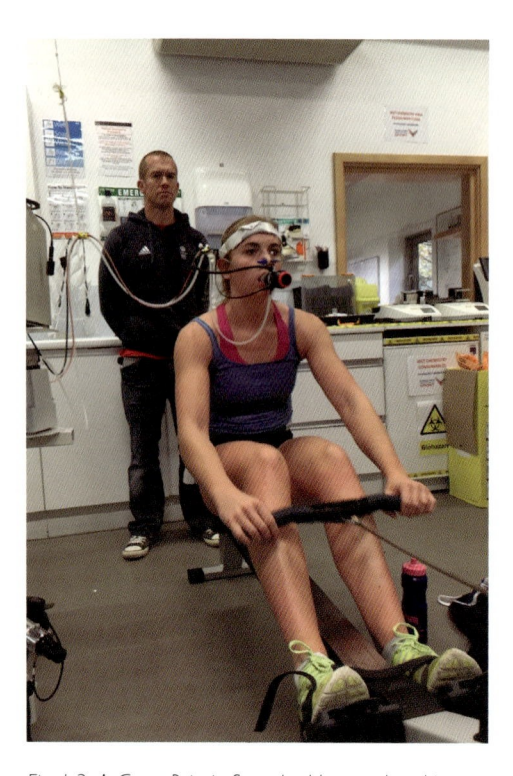

Fig. 1.3: A Great Britain Squad athlete undertaking a VO2 Max test under the watchful eye of Dr Mark Homer.

Rowers with larger muscle mass tend to have greater VO2s due to their ability to carry more blood through the extra muscle mass. Higher intensity, shorter duration aerobic training improves cardiac output and the rower's VO2.

The body's adaptation to low intensity aerobic training, or utilization training, will see it increase capillarization, the delivery of the oxygen to the muscle, and potentially increase blood volume.

Gaining extra lean muscle mass can be a difficult feat in a rower's training programme. The timing and sequencing of training, reducing the length of endurance sessions, and working out how the training is periodized as well as supported nutritionally are key factors in muscle gain. Weight training is an excellent tool here.

Training programme development

A training programme is driven by the factors that are needed to achieve the required performance. This is the starting point for any programme.

Once the end goal is stated, planning back from that point can begin. What is the end goal? A championship-winning peak programme will differ from the goal of earning as many points as possible over a season. The programme will be different for a long-distance head race or a 2,000m championship on the water or an ergometer test. Even the extra 112m at Henley Royal Regatta will need to be factored in.

All of these scenarios will require a different physiological load and energy system contribution. As the training sophistication of the rower increases, he will also need a more bespoke, individualized training focus within the programme.

Simplistically put, the programme should allow enough mobility work to respect

Performance, Training and Physiological Principles

the individual rower's anthropometric peculiarities, while enabling him to get into the positions that the technical model promotes. He needs to be strong enough to hold those positions and conditioned enough to maintain form under training and competition stress.

There are never any short cuts to performance or training. The rower and coach can train 'smarter', but there always needs to be hard training. Indeed, hard training generally needs to precede smart training. Training needs to prepare the rower physically, mentally and technically for the performance arena. The greater the number of quality strokes done in training, the greater number of winning strokes in racing.

Training priorities

High performance rowers

A precursor to high performance training is having the time to give to both training and recovery, so that the rower can adapt to his training. In an ideal world, by the time a rower enters the elite end of the sport he should have a level of conditioning that can maintain a training load that reflects his ambition. This will include a strong trunk that is well balanced in flexion as well as extension, and mobility through the hips and shoulder girdle. This conditioning will mean that the rower is able to hold his rowing form for the duration of long rowing sessions. Technically, a rower of this type will be rowing a long stroke that is leg-based, hip-driven and produces a strong distance per stroke. He will have the endurance base to be able to do at least two to three training sessions a day and be

Anaerobic Power
Anaerobic Threshold Power
Aerobic Power
Aerobic Fitness
Strength To Handle The Programme
Sound Fundamental Rowing Technique

Sequential Training Priority Hierarchy

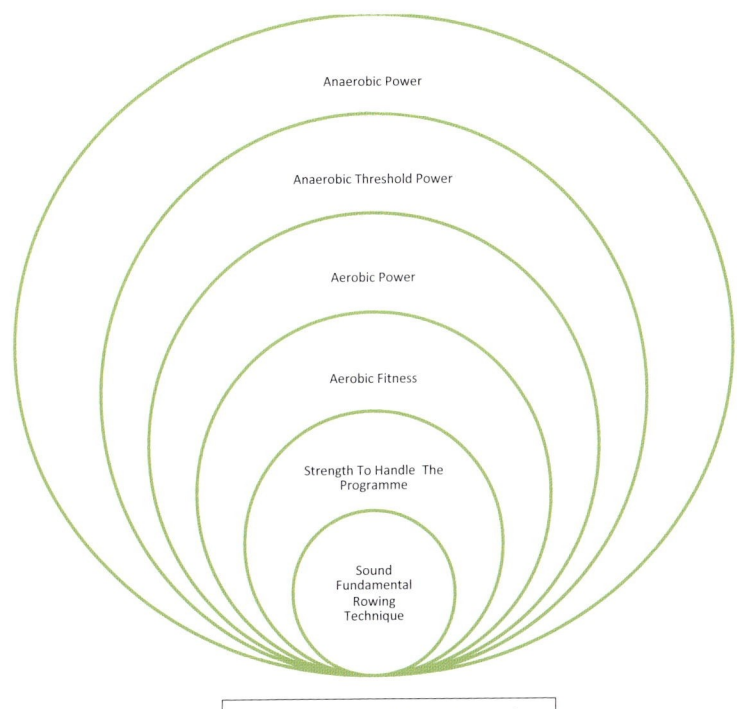

Fig. 1.4: Training hierarchy.

progressing physiologically for it. The old adage 'miles make champions' is true. The rower's physical capacity will be such that he can produce enough wattage per stroke to effectively move the boat at the speed he desires. To aspire for international success the rower must be able to do all this, as well as develop a mental model within his training to make sure he is getting the most out of the opportunities that training provides. This can be the solitude of long winter miles in a single, or emotionally challenging and competitive side-by-side training session after session.

Club rowers

Club rowers have to balance the time available for their training with a job or study commitments. When there is finite time as well as small opportunity to maximize recovery and training adaptation, prioritization of both crew and individual training needs is paramount. The physiological demands of racing are the same as for the elite rower but the training needs to be tailored to fit the club rower's commitments. This often means capitalizing on the opportunities provided by weekends, early mornings and late evenings, as well as lunchtimes and other points through the day when the rower can train. The coach and rower need to come up with novel solutions. If limited time is available on the water, club rowers should do a ladder of training intensities that challenges the various physiological training zones. This will often mean combining pieces of different lengths and intensities within one training session.

Club rowers should still spend time developing their conditioning to get the most out of the programme. Their programme will have a greater mix of training zones, although the principle of developing aerobic power will be the same as for elite rowers. For developing athletes within the club, the conditioning and technical side of the programme is a priority.

University rowers

A tremendous number of rowers take up the sport at university. The needs of the novice are different but no less important than those of a more established rower. University crews will often be a mix of those who rowed at school and those who are at entry level to the sport. Early stage programmes that have a strong technical and conditioning focus, working to a distance per stroke principle, not only provide the best opportunity for rowers to reach their early stage race goals but also set them up with sound principles to progress their rowing to a higher level. Quality coaching at this level can inspire a rower and give him the crucial grounding in sound technical principles that will set him on a path to not only enjoying the sport but performing well in university crews and beyond.

As with club rowers, there are a lot of competing demands on a student's time. Training needs to be balanced with academic commitments. For top-level university crews there also needs to be lateral thinking on how the training programme comes together to balance training requirements and academic needs. University rowers will be developing and their training needs to progress with their training base. Often a rower will produce an outstanding performance that is well ahead of his training background. As the training improves and stabilizes, rower and crew performance will become more consistent and repeatable.

School and junior rowers

School rowing programmes can develop very fast crews, and there are gifted coaches and strong programmes to be found in many schools. These are developmental by nature and nurture rowers from novice level to top national and international school and junior competitions. School rowers and juniors need to have schoolwork as a priority, but a strongly structured and technically focused training programme can allow them to achieve a lot in the sport and still attain top academic results. Run well, these programmes can give the rowers great life skills, from teamwork and time management to goal setting and achievement.

The training programme must engage the student, be diverse and facilitate a sound technical model, as well as develop the student's aerobic power. As a youngster matures it is advisable to sequence his training by developing the neural system and technical skills, the muscular and skeletal system, and then his aerobic power. Distance per stroke remains a fundamental principle.

Indoor rowers

Indoor rowers who are aiming to compete in indoor competitions have the same challenges as the outdoor rower. Ergometer training is very time efficient and convenient. The machines are very demanding. Fitness can come from aerobic training in gyms with other modalities, e.g. cycling, running and using cross-trainers. The load is greater on the ergometer than the water, particularly with stationary ergometers, so a strong and well-balanced strength programme is highly recommended.

Training priority principles

A rower must:

- Be robust and healthy enough to do the training programme.
- Have an endurance volume big enough to challenge and develop the aerobic pathways.
- Be powerful and strong enough to deliver the force required for each stroke.
- Have an anaerobic threshold level strong enough to deliver every stroke for the race.
- Hold technique at race pace.
- Have practised race strategies and tactics.

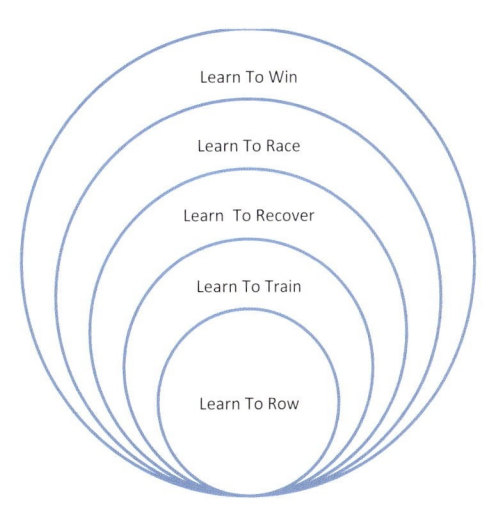

Fig. 1.5: Learning hierarchy.

A rower's programme needs to produce an environment that challenges him so he can learn and progress, understand himself, and develop as an athlete. He won't be able to do everything at once, so the programme needs to expose him to challenges and opportunities where he will develop his ability to train, recover, race and win.

Training programme development

Once the season's aims and objectives are decided, a programme that can deliver a performance of that level can be planned. What is required for the performance has to be considered against the current fitness, strength and conditioning and technical levels of the rower as well as his training age and level. Having a vision and order of how the physiology, technique and mental development of the rower's programme progresses is important. This can guide the coach and rower in making sure they are prioritizing the direction of the training to ensure the greatest performance gains.

Performance, Training and Physiological Principles

Rowing a 2,000m race or ergometer piece requires high endurance and strength levels to develop the rower's power. Often, training programmes in rowing are designed to achieve conflicting aims. Aiming for large strength or hypertrophy (muscle building) gains while in a large endurance phase has the potential to negate one or other of the training aims. This tends to happen in training programmes that are written in a concurrent manner. Sequentially written programmes allow for the rower to target a particular area of focus, measure improvement and develop it. Rowing is primarily an endurance sport so, not unsurprisingly, endurance training needs to take the majority of the programme's focus.

Each of the training blocks in a rower's programme needs to have a clear objective. If the training block is in a pre-season preparation phase that requires the rower to become stronger, then the training time, recovery time and focus given to that objective need to be enough to fulfill it.

The biggest gains made by a rower are the small incremental steps that are taken daily, stroke by stroke, lift by lift and step by step every session. The quality of what rowers do technically and physically, and the training and performance behaviours they develop on a daily basis, are what underpin the on-water or ergometer performance. This training discipline applies to the rowers' technical and 'boat feeling' improvements, adherence to stroke rate ceilings during training pieces, quick turns at the end of a training run to keep their heart rates up and to the quality of land training they do to support the water work. This is the backbone of a rowing crew or team's culture and should be expressed through the delivery of their training programme and training environment. The sooner these values, adherence and commitment to the training take place, the more confidence and commitment can come from the rowers. This raises the daily standard and it is through the preparatory phases of the programme that the building blocks of rowing performance are developed and major gains delivered.

Later chapters deal with the monitoring of training, which needs to be a vital part of performance development. The programme needs to reflect a variety of physiological levels: on-water technical work, aerobic training, anaerobic threshold training, oxygen transportation and anaerobic training. To get the most effective training stimulus it is important to monitor the rower to ensure he understands the physiological system he is working to, but also for the coach to know the rower is doing what he has planned for him to do. The rower needs to be able to do his steady training steadily, his fast training fast and over speed work over speed. Often in rowing, rowers overwork and go too hard at their long endurance work; by doing this they do not obtain the physiological adaptation that that particular type of endurance training can provide. There is also the danger that the rower is too fatigued or unable to technically achieve the higher pace work when required. Often when a rower gets into this situation there is a maladaptation to training and his physiology doesn't move on. The aim of long endurance training is to increase the muscles' ability to take oxygen from the blood through capillarization. This process allows for a more effective removal of by-products from the muscles' cells as well, lactic acid included. The higher the intensity, the less this adaptation occurs.

Recovery and contrasting the rower's training zones is important to allow the body the opportunity to adapt to the training stimulus. The training programme has to have enough variation and planning within it to allow for all the training zones to be accessed, with enough recovery for the rower to have the required training adaptation. Periodizing types of training (mixing anaerobic and aerobic) in the rower's

Performance, Training and Physiological Principles

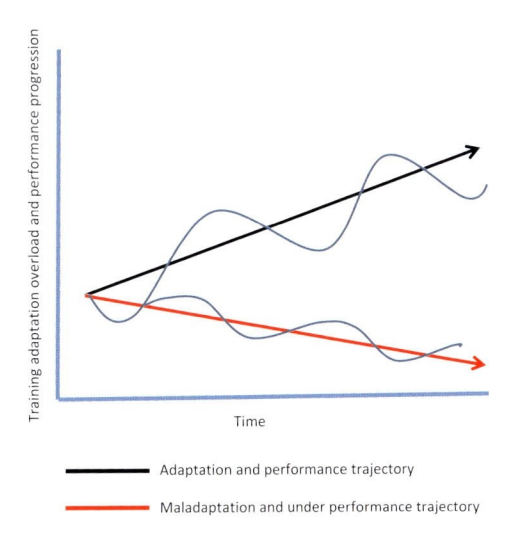

Fig. 1.6: Training overloading and maladaptation.

programme will give him the opportunity to stress his physiology as well as allow his body to regenerate physiologically stronger in that area. This is a process called overloading.

If the overloading phase continues for too long or the rower cannot get enough of the appropriate type of recovery, there can be a maladaptation to training where physiological progress stagnates or indeed regresses. Firstly, the rower becomes overstretched or overreached, then under-recovered or overtrained, which can be followed by illness. Aggressive unloading of training is important in these situations in order to stabilize the rower's basic physiology and then be able to slowly build him back to an appropriate level of training. The rower should be recording his daily resting heart rate and weight as a simple measure to monitor his readiness to train. Large fluctuations in either can be seen as an indication that the rower has not recovered properly from the previous training session or is harbouring an illness. This will help you ascertain the rower's readiness to train.

The following table is a good guide to connecting contrasting training zones with their physiological adaptations.

Zone	Stroke Rate per Minute	% of Gold Standard Time	% of Maximum Heart Rate	Approx. Lactate (Mmol)	Physiological Zone Definition
Utilization 3 (U3)	16–19	< 70%	65–75%	>1.5	Below the onset of blood lactate accumulation
Utilization 2 (U2)	16–19	65–77%	65–75%	>2	Below the onset of blood lactate accumulation
Utilization 1 (U1)	19–23	77–85%	70–80%	2–3	Above the onset of blood lactate accumulation but below the onset of metabolic acidosis
Anaerobic Threshold (AT)	23–28	85–88%	80–85%	3–4	Just below the onset of metabolic acidosis
Transport (TPT)	28–36	88–100%	85–95%	4+	Above the onset of metabolic acidosis
Anaerobic (AN)	36+	100%+	Max		Maximum effort

Fig. 1.7: Training matrix.

Performance, Training and Physiological Principles

Progression

The body works to a state of balance, or homeostasis, so the cycle of overloading and adaptation needs to be constantly applied and reviewed so the rower can keep developing his fitness. Increasing the duration, intensity or number of sessions, reducing the time between sets and adding extra sets are all ways that can overload the body and develop stronger physiology.

Cross-training

Many rowers do a variety of different sports to supplement their rowing training. It is a good opportunity to add some variation and different training stimuli, especially during the off-season. Running, swimming, canoeing, circuit work, ergometers and cycling are endurance activities that can benefit a rower's training. Another is cross-country skiing, an excellent all-body sport that is an especially popular cross-training activity in those countries that have alpine areas.

Cycling is a very good modality to develop base endurance and is probably the most popular cross-training activity for rowers. Rowers have been known to cross to cycling and be very successful; indeed Great Britain's Rebecca Romero was a silver medallist in rowing at the Athens Olympics and went into cycling to win a gold medal at the Beijing Games.

As it is leg-based only, cycling can be undertaken for longer periods than rowing sessions, and going over different terrain cycling allows for a large variation in the physiological stress that the rower can achieve from each training session. This is the advantage of cycling as a training modality when supplementing a traditional rowing programme. A lot of variety can be added to a cycling programme. Hill repeats can be used to strengthen legs. Undulating countryside can add good anaerobic threshold training, time trials build the rower's central cardiac system, and longer duration rides the aerobic utilization zone.

Cycling can also be done very effectively indoors on stationary bikes, turbo trainers or spinners.

Fig. 1.8: Great Britain Rowing Team members Sam Scrimgeour and Richard Chambers displaying good cycling skills.

TOP TIPS FOR ROWERS WHO CYCLE
- Be safe, check equipment, service your bike, obey road rules and wear a bike helmet.
- Ride in pairs rather than packs – you get more training and it's safer.
- Keep it to dry, low wind days.
- Get your bike set up to suit you.
- Be seen – have lights on front and back when you ride.

CHAPTER 2

TRAINING AND TECHNIQUE

Every rower has different physical attributes and proportions that need to be considered when he rows in a crew or is set up in his single scull. Quite often, different physical attributes can be 'rigged out' to help the crew achieve a similar stroke length, synchronization or timing of power application.

As coaches and rowers develop their technical model, they need to consider the physical principles of boat movement.

Leverage

The rowing boat moves forward by the rower using his oars to lever the boat through the water. There are three types of levers, and rowers use Class 1 and Class 2 types to move the boat.

As the rower grips the water at the beginning of the stroke, the effort of the Class 1 lever is at the handle of the oar, the fulcrum is at the rigger gate and pin, and the water creates the resistance of the lever. Once the rower has gripped the water with his spoon and the boat is accelerating, the movement becomes a Class 2 lever system where the effort is still in the oar handle, the force and fulcrum is on the spoon in the water, and the resistance is the drag from the hull being levered through the water.

Understanding how the boat is levered is fundamental to building a training programme. The taller the oarsman, the longer he is able to row. The more powerful the rower is, the further he can push the boat every stroke. These principles explain why successful rowers tend to be tall and powerful people. Indeed, length, power and stroke rate are the key ingredients of fast boats or ergometer scores. A rower's training priorities and programme need to reflect this.

Fig 2.1: Class 1 lever.

Training and Technique

Fig 2.2: Class 2 lever.

Stroke cycle

To lever the boat using the Class 1 and 2 levers, the rower must then take his oar out of the water at the finish of the drive phase of the stroke and return to the catch to take the next stroke. This produces a drive/recovery impulse movement of the hull. This is quite unique to rowing boats and provides the rower with his greatest challenge: to feel for the boat and move in harmony and balance, providing a rhythm to the hull and crew.

Drive phase

The timing of the two changes of direction is crucial to optimizing a rower's effective length. The change of direction at the front turn, where the rower moves from the recovery phase to the drive phase, is crucial to connecting the rower with the oar's spoon, the water and the boat. The connection between the spoon, the water and the rower's power through his feet links the elements of the system together, i.e. the rower, the oar and the boat. This connection gives an initial acceleration to the hull. As part of the drive/recovery impulse, this is the area of the stroke where the boat is moving with the lowest hull velocity. The rower needs to quickly accelerate the boat at this point so that the velocity of the hull is maintained at a higher level and therefore produces a higher average speed. As this is the point of the stroke cycle with the lowest boat speed, it is therefore the point of the stroke cycle that requires the greatest load for the rower to move and generate acceleration into the system. To do this, the rower needs to dominate the first half of the drive with his leg strength, engaging his gluteal muscles at the catch and using his strong hamstrings and quadriceps to accelerate the hull. The earlier the rower can drive his heels into the foot stretcher, the earlier his gluteal engagement will occur. Therefore, the technical model should include a leg-initiated and dominated drive. This power needs to be applied while he is rowing a continuous stroke cycle after the blade is in the water, otherwise the rower's power is pushing the boat backward as it is not connected to the blade.

Once the boat is up and accelerating, the rower will need to open his trunk off his legs to keep the force increasing on the blade and the hull accelerating further over the whole stroke. Just after the blade leaves the water at the finish of the drive phase, the boat's velocity is at its highest level. The mechanics of the boat's velocity do vary between low endurance stroke

Training and Technique

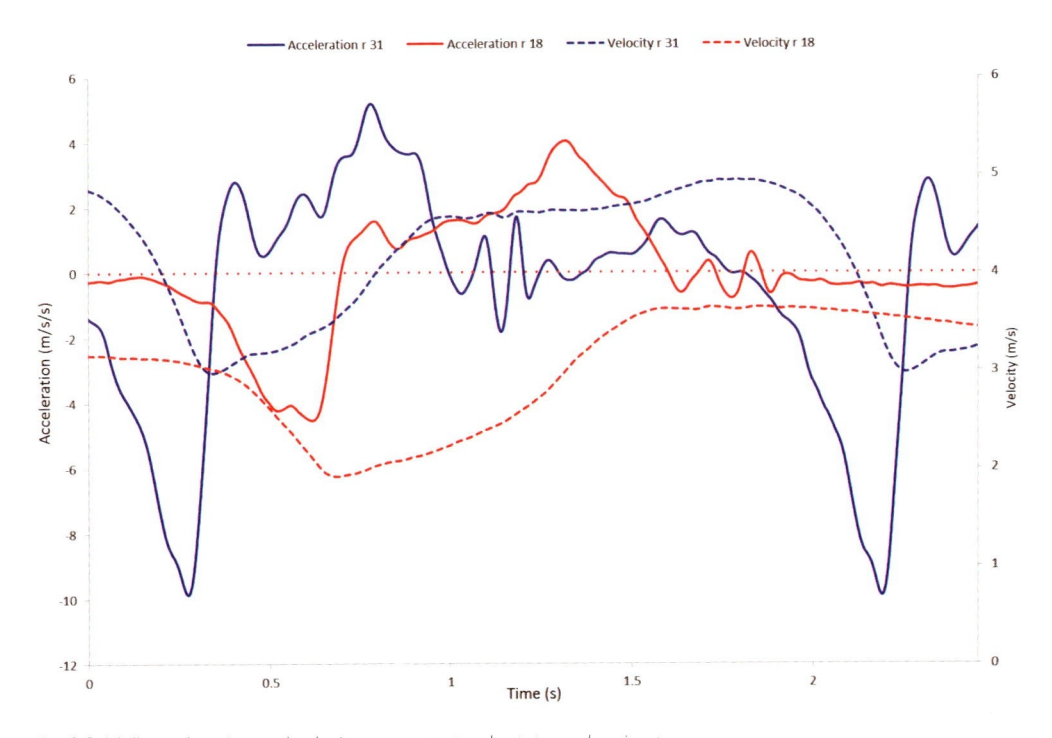

Fig. 2.3: Hull acceleration and velocity traces at steady state and racing pace.

rates and higher race rates. As the stroke rate increases, there is not enough time for the boat velocity to slow down as much and to maintain a higher velocity the rower needs to 'pick the boat up' quicker and earlier in the drive. This creates a steeper delivery of force by the rower, producing a steeper and higher initial acceleration on the hull. Fig. 2.3 demonstrates the hull dynamics changing between low rate endurance training and high rate race work.

As the rower spends time pushing against the water with his blade during the drive phase, there comes a point at which he cannot drive his oar through the water any quicker and looks to take less time on the recovery, thereby increasing his stroke rate to increase his speed. This usually occurs somewhere around stroke rate 22–26.

There is a balance between power or distance per stroke and stroke rate that needs to be included in a rower's training programme. This ratio between the drive and recovery phases delivers the rower's and boat's rhythm. In low rate endurance training, the ratio is nearly 1:3 drive:recovery, and when racing is more like 1:1. To train for a technical model that is leg-based and hip-driven requires attention not only to the large leg muscles and hip complex, but also the trunk, which must be strong enough to transfer the force from the legs and hips and out through the lats (latissimus dorsi) and arms to the handle of the oars. Quite often, rowers' lower abdominals, obliques and lower back muscles are not strong enough to take the body's load. Apart from leaking suspension and load through the drive, rowers can also make themselves vulnerable to injury. This area of training is covered in later chapters. As has been demonstrated above, it is important for the correct body position and drive sequence to be held so that the rower may utilize his biggest and most powerful muscles to move the boat when its velocity is lower, through to the smaller muscle groups (arms) when the acceleration is maximized.

Recovery phase

The finish of the stroke is the connection between the drive phase and the recovery phase. This is the part of the stroke cycle where you want to maximize the highest boat velocity. The finish position of the rower is important to optimize his recovery. He needs to have his legs pressed out against the footboard, shoulders behind his seat, elbows high and be feeling he is maintaining pressure on the spoon until the natural clean release of the spoon from the water. Anatomically he should be squeezing and pressing through his gluteal muscles, set through his lower abdomen, and sitting on the back of his sit bones (ischial tuberosity). He needs to keep this press through the foot-stretcher as the spoon is released from the water and the hands bring the handle around the finish with the speed of the hull. The action of the rower's gluteal muscles squeezing in and drawing down his lower abdominals allows for a pelvic tilt or rockover, with the rower's position on his seat moving to the front of his sit bones and his weight going low into his feet. At this point, the rower's arms are straight and loose and his shoulders are in front of the seat.

Posture

There is often a great debate about posture and 'sitting up' – its value and importance. Posture can be a misunderstood term. Relaxation is key in a good rowing rhythm, and quite often rowers mistake a rigid and straight thoracic (upper) spine as good posture. If a rower has a good drive and recovery sequence as described above, is trained to have length in his hip flexors and hamstrings as well as strength in his lower abdominals and gluteal muscles, the rockover will come from the pelvis and not be a hinge further up the back. This allows for good length and trunk extension from the hip, providing a natural and relaxed thoracic back position. Good posture comes from the pelvis and lumbar spine, below the level that a belt is worn.

Points of connection with the boat and ergometer

There are three contact points the rower has with the rowing system: handle, foot-stretcher and seat. For the most effective rowing, it is important that the rower has the most effective connection with these points. The rower's grip needs to be relaxed with not too much use of the wrists for squaring or feathering. The correct foot-stretcher angle needs to be found so that the rower can utilize the whole of the soles of his feet during the drive phase, and he needs to be able to sit properly on the seat as this maximizes the drive and recovery sequences.

Seating position

When the rower sits down on the seat with his legs flat, he should be able to feel he is sitting on the front (anterior) of his sit bones. He should be able to feel this position on the seat from where he has rocked over from the finish with weight in his feet, through the recovery and the front turn, as well as for the first two thirds of the drive phase, where he is pushing predominantly with his legs. When he aggressively opens his trunk, his seating position will change to feel he is sitting on the back (posterior) of his sit bones. He will be in this position on the seat through the finish as he presses out and the handle leads him out through the finish and back onto the front of his seat. This sequencing will be part of the boat's rhythm. The aim should be that the rower is able to keep his pelvis and lumbar spine in line at the same angle through the rockover. This angle or lumbar pelvic ratio would ideally be 1:1.

Grip

To produce accurate blade work in sculling or rowing, the grip needs to be very relaxed. In all the boats, to maximize leverage the hands need to be at the end of the handles in sculling, and the outside hand needs to be on the end of the handle in sweep rowing.

Sweep rowing grip

When the rower is sitting in the finish position, he needs to be rotating through his thoracic upper spine so that he can still be sitting centrally on the seat and pushing through both his feet. He needs to lead away with the outside arm, letting the inside arm follow, with a low inside shoulder. This will result in the rower having relaxed and natural 'hands away'. The outside hand needs to be at the end of the handle, with the inside hand at least 2.5 thumb lengths apart. As the rower comes in towards the front turn, he needs to square and place with the inside hand, arching the thumb up and the fingers down with a small amount of wrist. The outside hand loops around and hangs from the catch. The wrists are flat and the elbows draw straight through and stay high at the finish. With the rower's weight in the bows at the finish of the stroke, he needs to feel the elbows are staying high to keep providing load to his blade in the water in the last part of the drive. Through the drive phase, the knuckle (metacarpophalangeal joint) should be as close to 90° as possible, similar to a monkey grip.

Handle size is important in sweep rowing. If the handle is too big, the grip becomes ineffective and forearm injuries can develop. If the grip is too small, it also becomes ineffective. Therefore, the rower should ensure that his hand can fit loosely around the handle with the thumb to the forefinger approximately a centimetre apart.

Sculling grip

With sculling, it is important to keep the thumbs on the end of the handles, and the first

Fig. 2.4: Great Britain's 2014 World Championship bronze medal-winning lightweight men's four displaying a good relaxed hang on the handles.

23

Training and Technique

Fig. 2.5: Great Britain's World Championship single sculling representative Victoria Thornley demonstrating a good sculling grip, with her fingers close to the end of the handle and good thumb control.

set of knuckles at 90°. As with sweep rowing, handle size is important so that the thumb and fingers can do the squaring and feathering with less wrist. A flat wrist during the drive, following the elbow, makes for a flat path of the spoon in the water. High elbows at the finish are also necessary to keep the press and push on the blade in the water, as the bow of the boat is lower at the finish of a stroke and the blade can wash out of the water, shortening the drive phase.

Technical excellence

Olympic and World Champions Helen Glover (left) and Heather Stanning (right) are excellent technical role models, with an immense feel for the boat and sound technical principles.

Placement

Fig. 2.6: The change of direction of the rower and the spoon at the front turn of the stroke is the most difficult to time. The rower needs to have the patience and relaxation to let the boat come all the way to them during the final stages of the recovery and time the entry of the blade to the water. Timed well, the blade takes the water and the rower can then apply his full power from a long forward position.

Training and Technique

Catch

Fig. 2.7: The rower catches the boat through the feet using his gluteal muscles and quadriceps to initiate the drive and produce the initial acceleration of the hull in the drive phase.

Early drive

Fig. 2.8: Displaying a long relaxed hang through the arms and latissimus dorsi muscles, set and connected through their abdominals and trunk, allow Heather (right) and Helen (left) to have an extremely effective early leg drive to keep their boat accelerating sharply from the catch.

Mid drive

Fig. 2.9: With a long leg drive Heather and Helen are also showing a loose, straight arm, well connected hang. They are commencing working their trunk off their legs to keep the sweep and acceleration on the boat by using their drive sequences. The drive phase is very horizontal, connected by the two rowers who are very well suspended between the hands and the feet. This allows them to maximize the amount of power they can apply to the water on the face of the spoon. The picture shows this with the mound of water visible ahead of the spoon.

25

Training and Technique

Late drive

Fig. 2.10: In a very strong position late in the drive, Heather and Helen still have their arms straight while the legs and trunk have nearly finished their drive. An aggressive hip opening at this point allows the power to continue to build on the blade and velocity on the hull. The shoulders are engaged while the arms are straight.

Finish

Fig. 2.11: With the legs and trunk finished, the shoulders initiate the arm draw. As the weight of the rowers is now in the bows, the boat is lower in the water and the rowers need to draw their arms high to keep the spoons buried and the power on the face of the spoon. Heather and Helen have high elbow positions; power is being applied to the face of the blade, with a mound of water on its face and a cavity behind it.

Finish and release

Fig. 2.12: The stroke finds its natural finish with a strong leg press against the foot-stretcher. When the pressure is released the handle can be tapped down and the spoon steps out of the cavity, which has been created through the drive, behind the blade.

Training and Technique

Finish and feather

Fig. 2.13: As the blade has been released from the water the rowers' inside wrists can feather the oar and the blade becomes parallel to the water, reducing wind resistance against it during the recovery. As Heather and Helen demonstrate, their finish position has been maintained to maximize the run of the boat off the finish of the stroke. It is a good gathering position to then lead with the hands and, moving with the boat, commence the recovery phase.

Early recovery

Fig. 2.14: Without being stiff or tight, the rowers lead with their hands, release their knees and rockover, transferring their weight from the seat to their feet. Heather and Helen, early in their recovery, are swinging through very relaxed and about to come onto their feet.

Mid recovery

Fig. 2.15: The recovery sequences are mirror images of the drive sequences. Having come onto the feet early in the recovery, Heather and Helen have been well organized in the first quarter of the recovery to be almost in the catch position and can read and maximize the run of the boat.

Training and Technique

Late recovery

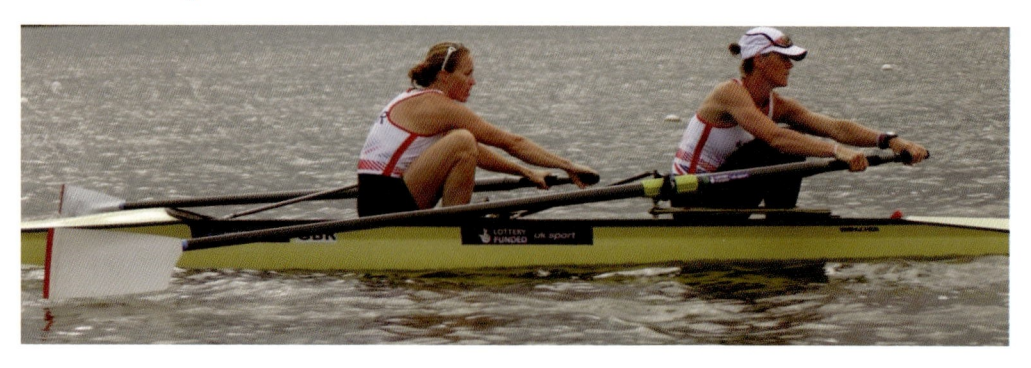

Fig. 2.16: Having organized themselves into the catch position early in the recovery, Heather and Helen can read the boat and, as part of their rhythm through the front turn, have squared the blade and are preparing to 'land' on the blades as the last part of their recovery phase and place the blade.

Common faults

Poor sequencing/drive phase and bum shoving

'Bum shoving' is a common problem for rowers, and very common in beginners. The rower does not connect the water or the ergometer cog with the handle or chain through his body to the footboard, so that when he pushes his legs, the handle moves slowly and the rower's bottom shoots quickly through the drive without connection to it or suspension through his hands and feet.

Coaching cues:
- Look for a better connection between the handle and the feet at the catch.
- See that the handle and seat move back from the catch together.
- Start the body drive earlier.

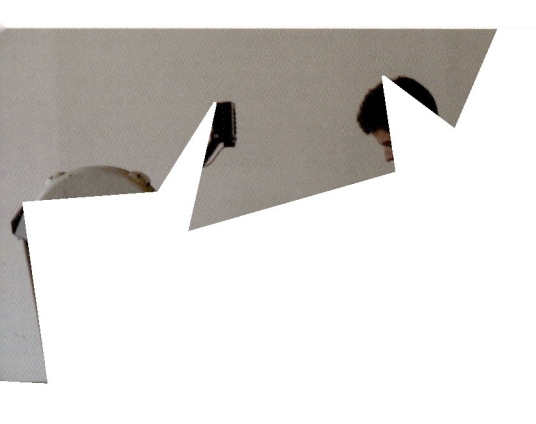

Fig. 2.17: 'Bum shoving'.

Training and Technique

Fig. 2.18: Opening the trunk too early.

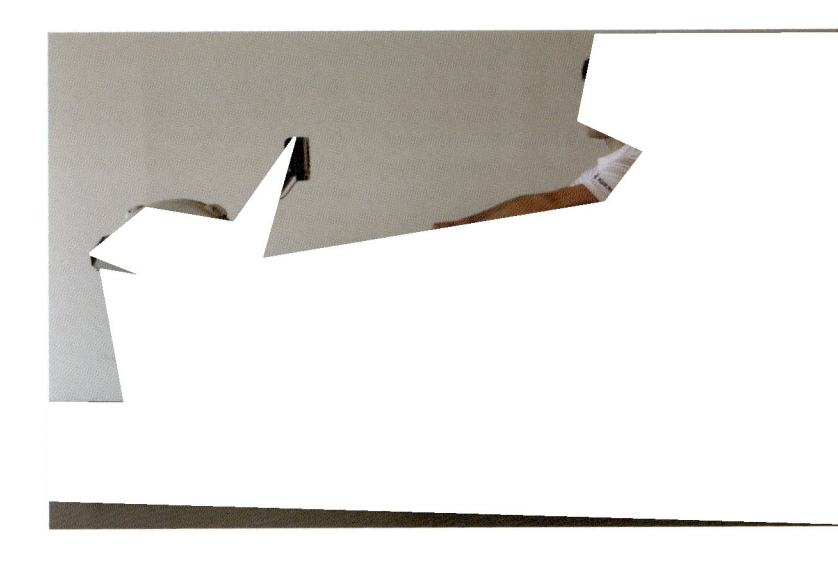

Opening the trunk too early

If a rower mistimes his arrival at front, stopping and taking too much time with his change of direction, there is a tendency for the trunk to open too early, devaluing the power that can be produced by the big leg muscles. This can be a problem with novice rowers, but can make its way to higher levels too. Ideally, the legs dominate for the first two thirds of the drive, and the trunk opens aggressively to keep the hull accelerating in the last third.

Coaching cues:
- Reinforce the drive sequence of legs, body and arms.
- Reinforce the recovery sequence of arms, body and slide.
- Try pause rowing to correct sequences.

Arms too early

In a well-timed and executed drive, the legs have picked up the boat and put acceleration into the hull in the first two thirds of the drive. The trunk opens aggressively in the last third, engaging the shoulders then finishing with the arms. So, the big muscles are used to put the acceleration into the hull and the smaller groups maintain the handle acceleration. Often rowers start using their arms before their shoulders have engaged, consequently losing the power the shoulders can provide. The rower ends up pulling himself onto the handle rather than pushing the boat away at the finish.

Coaching cues:
- Straight arm rowing, only using legs and body.
- Build stroke sequences with 'legs only' strokes, legs and bodies, then bring in the arms.
- Check recovery sequences to see that the rower is 'organizing' himself from the back turn to set himself up for the change of direction at the front turn and the drive phase and sequences.

Asymmetries

People have individual anatomical quirks – leg length differences are quite common occurrences. Whether they are real or perceived leg length differences, they can produce shearing

29

Training and Technique

Fig. 2.19: Arms too early.

Fig. 2.20: Olympic silver medallist and former World Champion Chris Bartley demonstrating one-arm one-leg rowing.

forces through the rower. A right leg shorter than the left can see the rower compensating by pulling up with a high left shoulder, or indeed driving across the boat or over to the side on an ergometer seat. When a coach or rower finds himself faced with this situation, orthotics and manipulation of the rig can be very useful.

It is best to seek a professional review, e.g. from a physiotherapist.

Rowing with one hand on the handle and only the opposite leg allows the rower to balance himself and either find symmetry or identify a weakness that can be addressed in the gym or with the help of a physiotherapist.

Training and Technique

Stroke correction

Having explained the rationale of the technical model and described some common faults, the following exercises and drills are aimed at providing you with some ideas on how to improve your rowing and rectify any faults. They cover three key areas: sequences, position and suspension.

Rockover

The rower sits on the front (anterior) of his sit bones (ischial tuberosity) on the seat in the boat. He should feel that when he moves into the finish position, he comes over onto the tips of his sit bones. He rocks over from the front to the back, then from the back to the front, maintaining pressure against the footplate by activating the gluteal and quadricep muscles. Then, he rocks from the forward position to the finish position by utilizing the abdominal muscles and hips. He swings back over forward from the finish position by keeping the press through the legs and drawing in the lower abdominals.

This exercise starts with straight arms, moves to bringing the arm movement in and then out to three-quarters of the slide off the recovery. A nice lumbar/pelvic rhythm develops and the rower can increase complexity by increasing the cadence while holding good form. When done properly, this exercise also demonstrates how the boat moves towards the bow when the rockover is well-timed and executed.

Coaching cues:
- Rock over below the level of the belt.
- Relax the thoracic spine and shoulders.
- Feel the boat move to the bow with the rhythm of the sequence.

Blades on the water

Taking the boat's balance out of the equation allows the rower to concentrate on what particular part of the stroke sequence he needs to address or reinforce.

Blades on the water can start from the rockover exercise previously mentioned. This allows the rower to achieve a rockover with relaxation in his upper body. As the rower builds out to full slide he starts taking strokes while he feathers the blade onto the water at the finish, and only takes the blade off the water and squares very late, therefore the spoon is on the water for as much of the recovery as possible. By alternating strokes that are loaded (blades in the water) and unloaded (blades out of the water/'fresh air' strokes) the rower is able to feel sequence and load and better understand how stroke sequencing helps to develop hull acceleration as well.

When the rower is proficiently displaying the correct rockover and drive phase, with a leg-dominated drive, the hips' through position should be close to the half-drive position. Complexity can be added where the rower alternates having the blades on the water with having the blades off the water, thereby looking to hold the stroke sequences and balance the boat. Start with square blades and then move to feathered.

Coaching cues:
- Unfold the blade onto the water at the finish so the boat is stable.
- Coach sequences with arms, the rower rocking over to get his body forward then sliding up the slide.
- Emphasize relaxation during the recovery.
- Maintain relaxation and sequence during loaded strokes.

Paused rowing

Paused rowing is an under-utilized stroke correction tool. Its benefits include encouraging the rower to feel for the boat, honing his and the crew's sequence timing, and it is a great tool to correct the boat's balance.

Training and Technique

Figs 2.21, 2.22 and 2.23: Olympic Champion and six times World Champion Katherine Grainger (left) and World Championship medallist Victoria Thornley (right) demonstrating the rockover exercise.

Training and Technique

Fig. 2.24: Pauses can also be included to help trunk training and correct muscle sequencing during the recovery.

Paused rowing can be done at many parts of the recovery. The most common position is quarter-slide from the finish, where the rower should have his weight on his feet, arms straight and shoulders forward of the seat.

Adding multiple slide pausing positions during a single recovery helps the rower feel for the boat's run, but also allows the coach to be able to check the rower's sequencing and positions at that particular part of the stroke.

Pauses can be just as valuable on the ergometer as they are on the water.

With feet out, the rower pauses at the finish with the arms away straight and blades off the water. The rower checks his finish position and makes sure he is squeezing through his gluteal muscles and is thus giving himself a leg press against the foot-stretcher. He can then lift one leg, then the other, while drawing in his lower abdominal muscles. Having mastered this, he can then add complexity by taking alternate hands off the handles and touching his nose while lifting his feet. This is a very good exercise to be done on the ergometer as part of the rower's trunk training.

Coaching cues:
- Check that the boat is being pushed level off the finish so that the rowers are 'on top' of the boat and able to balance the boat at the pause.
- Check that time is taken to feel the run of the boat and for the crew to move out of the pause together.
- As the boat is moving slower after the longer recovery time with the pause, use the run out and glide of the boat at the pause to time the change of direction at the front turn and pick up the boat with good hand/feet timing.

Double finishes

This exercise is done with unloaded fresh air strokes at (a) arms away, (b) arms and trunk, and (c) quarter-slide. The aim of the exercise is to feel for the run of the boat and for the rower to isolate what muscles he uses and how he sequences both the drive and recovery into and out of the finish in both a loaded (oars in the water) and unloaded (oars coming through the air) manner.

Training and Technique

Check that the rower is sitting in the correct finish position, as previously described in the rockover exercise. During the drive phase guide him to feel the draw through his lats and biceps, and through his triceps and the stretching of his lats during the recovery. As he builds out from the finish he is also able to practise his lumbar/pelvic rhythm on the seat. By squeezing his gluteal muscles and drawing in with his lower abdominals he will be able to rockover through his hips from the finish of the stroke and have his weight transfer onto his feet, also working the last quarter of the drive phase using his back off his driving legs.

By alternating these strokes with full rowing strokes, the rower is able to feel for the unloaded movement and range and then apply it to the full strokes. This exercise is also good for feeling for the run of the boat during the double finish and relaxing with it. As the boat is running out for a long time, the rower is well placed to take advantage of the exercise to practise and hone the timing of his glide on the slide and the timing of his blade entry at the placement.

Coaching cues:
- Do the exercise with alternating loaded and fresh air strokes, looking for the same freedom of movement under load as when unloaded during the fresh air stroke.
- In sculling keep leading with the left hand and in-sweep with the outside arm.
- Build the rhythm of the crew through the back turn and the timing of the arrival at the front turn without putting extra weight into the stern.

Wide and narrow grip

Wide-grip in-sweep rowing, or sculling with the hands down the loom of the sculls, is a valuable exercise to check that the rower is connecting and hanging through his lats during the drive phase. Having a wider grip means that the load to the rower is increased as he is working closer to the fulcrum of the lever.

With the shoulders set down low and the rower hanging through his arms and lats, the upper body needs to allow power transmission through from the power-producing legs, hips and back.

A variation in sweep boats and on the ergometer is to row with the hands close together. This is a less powerful position but challenges the rower to be set in the right position and hang through the drive.

Coaching cues:
- Keep the pressure on so that the blade interaction with the water is the same as in normal rowing.
- Try different hand widths to change the load on the rower as a variation.
- Roll the elbows outward to feel more of a hang through the lats.

Shoulder stabilization and upper body strength is often overlooked in training programmes. It is especially important for female rowers.

Fig. 2.25: Narrow grip.

Training and Technique

Suspension and push back strokes

The key to good and fast rowing is a rower's ability to suspend his body weight between the oar handles and the foot-stretcher and apply his power. When lighter and smaller rowers beat heavier and taller rowers it's usually because they have more effectively suspended their body weight, applied their power efficiently and moved well with the boat in the recovery. To effectively suspend his body weight and apply his power the rower needs to be moving well with the boat during the recovery phase so that he can judge the timing of the blades entering the water and 'catching' the boat through his feet. Timed well, the skilful rower applies his power against the spoon when the boat moves forward. If he mistimes his power application before the blades are in the water, the boat kicks back and the rower will feel a heavy boat. There are exercises that can be done to improve the change of direction of the rower at the front turn, and also improve his quality of suspension.

Sitting three-quarters forwards with the blades square and buried in the water, the rower 'backs' the boat down. This pushes the boat towards the stern. As the boat is moving backwards when the rower changes direction at the catch, there is a greater load on the blade and the rower can almost stand up as he suspends between his hands (handle and blade) and his feet. He should be encouraged to get his heels pushing through the footboard as early as he can to better activate his gluteal muscles and get his body weight suspended. Once the rower is proficient with this he can reduce the length on the slide and time at the front to get his suspension. After feeling his suspension on the first stroke he can build up to two, three and four strokes. As the boat is moving forwards and increasing in velocity, the rower needs to judge his change of direction at the front turn to have his hands leading his feet and to maintain the quality of suspension he got on the first stroke.

A variation of this can be done on the ergometer. It is often best to introduce and reinforce ideas and technical focuses on the ergometer before heading out onto the water. Tying a boat tie or piece of rope to the handle of the ergometer and threading it through its head allows the coach to stop the handle and determine the load on the rower. By doing this the rower can feel a similar quality of suspension to that which he felt on the water in the exercise described above. The advantage the ergometer has is that the coach can physically manipulate and coach the rower to explain what he wants the rower to achieve. Of course, always ask the rower if it is OK to touch him.

The same exercise can be done in the rowing tank. The tank is a great tool for coaches to be able to explain and manipulate the rower to make technical changes. The mirrors around the tank provide valuable instant visual feedback for the rower.

The rower should be drawing in his lower abdominal muscles, using his gluteals and hanging through his lats while his shoulders are nice and relaxed. This is the connected feel the rower should be looking for as he takes the catch and gets a good quality of suspension. This exercise can also be used to strengthen, in a very sport-specific way, the gluteal and lower abdominal muscles. How long can the rower hold the correct suspended position? You can move the exercise out in 15-second chunks as strength and endurance improve.

Just as the quality of suspension is important at the beginning of the stroke, it is also as important to maintain it through the whole of the drive phase. Back-end suspension can also be done on the water and the ergometer, with 'arms only' suspension, trunk and arms, quarter-slide and half-slide. The drive sequence of legs, hips, shoulders then arms is key in getting

Training and Technique

Figs 2.26, 2.27 and 2.28: Suspension – front, middle and back.

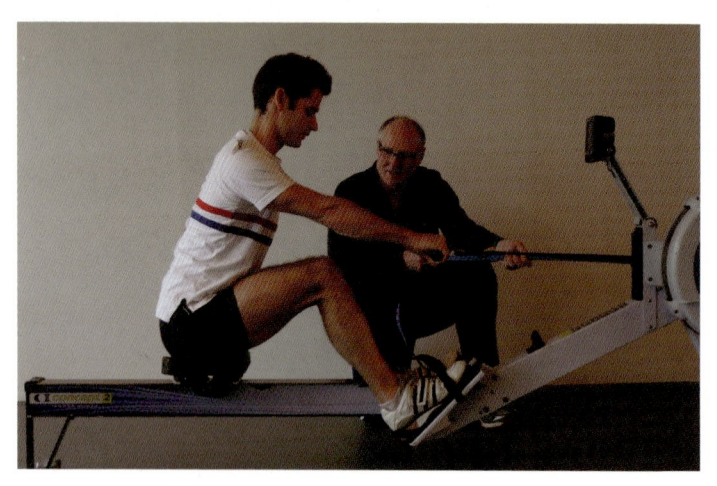

Training and Technique

Fig. 2.29: Suspension in a rowing tank.

and maintaining a good quality of suspension in the later part of the stroke. When doing these exercises on the water, a bungee or sea anchor placed around the hull adds extra resistance so that the rower can feel and develop his quality of suspension.

Coaching cues:
- Practise suspension at the catch, mid drive and finish.
- Hang from the handle.
- Keep feeling the hang as the boat speed increases.

Fig. 2.30: Finish suspension on water.

CHAPTER 3

ROWING TRAINING

Balance

Balance and variety are key components of any training programme and will give the rower training stimulus, technical improvements, competitive and mental training as well as the motivation to succeed. The best rowing technician without a fitness level will not succeed; however, a high proficiency of technical ability will mean that the rower can produce better, more effective and efficient strokes during his training. Holding his concentration and form as the load and fatigue increase during training sessions is key for racing preparation. Time permitting, it is often best to have a strong technically focused session on the water and have the rower's primary fitness work on land until he is able to get the most out of his on-water training sessions. This land training could be rowing-specific on the ergometer or, for less experienced rowers, on a stationary bike, or cycling, running, or circuit work.

Variety

Within the physiological training zones, imaginative sessions can help develop the rower's rhythm but also keep challenging the rower's training stimulus and adaptation. Pyramids, castles and rate builds are all good ways of adding variety and challenge to a rower's training.

A pyramid is where the training pieces reduce in time and then increase in time. Often the intensity increases then decreases. For example:

5min stroke rate 24 / 4min stroke rate 26 / 3min stroke rate 28 / 2min stroke rate 30 / 1min stroke rate 32 / 2min stroke rate 30 / 3min stroke rate 28 / 4min stroke rate 26 / 5min stroke rate 24

A castle is where the rates and intensity rise and fall. This type of training is very good for the development of the boat's rhythm. For example:

3 × 2min stroke rate 28 / 2min stroke rate 24 / 2min stroke rate 28 / 2min stroke rate 24 / 2min stroke rate 28 / 2min stroke rate 24

Sample workouts

Aerobic

Aerobic utilization training stroke rate range is 16 to 24.

Steady state

12km continuous rowing at a stroke rate between 16 and 20

16km continuous rowing at a stroke rate between 16 and 20

20km continuous rowing at a stroke rate between 16 and 20

Aerobic continuous training is the opportunity to perfect and hone technique and perform technical exercises. Alactic sprints (6–10 strokes) can also be done to help fire the neural pathways and make the aerobic training interesting.

Stroke rate play with castles and pyramids can also help develop the boat's rhythm. 20- to 30-minute blocks can be used to add variation. Examples include:

Rowing Training

2min, 3min or 5min changes at stroke rate 20/18/16/18/20

2min, 3min or 5min changes at stroke rate 20/16/20/16/20

2min, 3min or 5min changes at stroke rate 19/21/23/19

2min, 3min or 5min changes at stroke rate 23/21/19/23

2min, 3min or 5min changes at stroke rate 23/19/21/23

Flat stroke rate pieces at rates between 16 and 23, holding consistent pace

4 × 2,000m with 500m stroke rate changes at:

Stroke rate 19/21/23/19

Stroke rate 23/21/19/23

Stroke rate 23/19/21/23

Anaerobic threshold

The anaerobic threshold training stroke rate range is 24 to 28. The time of this zone lasts between 7 and 20 minutes. Anaerobic threshold can be crudely classified as the pace the rower can go when he goes as hard as he can for 20 minutes. This area is below race rate and the base race rhythm is well developed in this training zone. Therefore, flat rates holding pace and rate-variable pieces can be used to challenge and develop the boat's rhythm.

4 × 10min at flat stroke rates; stroke rates 24/26/26/28

5 × 10min with 5-minute steps:

Stroke rate 24

Stroke rate 24/26

Stroke rate 26

Stroke rate 26/28

Stroke rate 28

3 × 15min with stroke rate steps every 5 minutes:

5min changes at stroke rate 24/26/28

5min changes at stroke rate 26/24/26

5min changes at stroke rate 28/26/28

4 × 7min:

2 × stroke rate 26

2 × stroke rate 28

3 × 2,000m pieces with stroke rate steps at 1,000m and 1,500m (1,000m/500m/500m):

Stroke rate 24/26/24

Stroke rate 26/28/26

Stroke rate 26/28/28

2 × 5,000m at rates 24 and 26

2 × 5,000m at flat stroke rates of 26 and 28

3 × 20min at flat stroke rates of 24, 26 and 24

Transportation training

Transportation training develops the central cardiac system and develops the rower's boat rhythm at and just below race stroke rate. Transportation training's duration is between 3 and 7 minutes.

4 × 7min with stroke rate steps at 3 and 5 minutes (3 minutes/2 minutes/2 minutes) with 7 to 10 minutes between sets:

Stroke rate 28/30/32

Stroke rate 30/32/34

4 × 4min with stroke rate steps at 2 minutes and 3 minutes (2 minutes/1 minute/1 minute):

Stroke rate 28/30/32

Stroke rate 30/32/34

Stroke rate 32/34/36

4 × 4min with stroke rate steps at 1 minute and 2 minutes (1 minute/1 minute/2 minutes):

Stroke rate 28/30/32

Stroke rate 30/32/34

Stroke rate 32/34/36

5 × 3min with two sets at stroke rate steps at 1 minute and 2 minutes (1 minute/1 minute/1 minute) and the last piece with a flat rate:

Rowing Training

2 × stroke rate 32/34/36

2 × stroke rate 34/36/38

1 × stroke rate 36/36/36

3 × 2,000m with stroke rate steps at 1,000m and 1,500m (1,000m/500m/500m):

2 × rate 30/32/34

1 × rate 32/34/36

4 × 1,500m with stroke rate steps at 500m and 1,000m (500m/500m/500m):

Stroke rate 30/32/30

Stroke rate 32/30/32

Stroke rate 32/34/32

Stroke rate 32/32/32

3–6 × 1,000m racing; can either be done at race pace from a start, mid pace or building speed

2–4 × 1,250m racing; can either be done at race pace from a start, mid pace or building speed

2–3 × 1,500m racing; can either be done at race pace from a start, mid pace or building speed

Anaerobic training

By definition anaerobic training is where the intensity of work sets are high and the rower is working his physiology system above the energy level that oxygen can provide. The following sample workloads are divided into a group that can develop the rower's capacity to tolerate and produce anaerobic power, as well as short alactic pieces that are so short they utilize the creatine phosphate energy system that is stored in the muscle cells and neither develop lactic acid nor stress the aerobic system.

Anaerobic capacity training

12 × 1min with 1 to 1 minute 30 seconds rest between pieces, with the work at a stroke rate of <36

12 × 250m with 1 to 1 minute 30 seconds rest between pieces, with the work at a stroke rate of <36

12 × 250m with 1 to 1 minute 30 seconds rest between pieces, with the work at a stroke rate of <36, with a sea anchor or bungee attached to the hull to add extra drag to the boat for the rowers to work against

12 × 100m with maximum rate and 30 seconds off between pieces

4 × 100m on, 100m off / 250m on, 100m off / 500m on, 100m off, at or above race rate

4 × 10 strokes racing, 20 strokes off / 20 strokes racing, 20 strokes off / 30 strokes racing, 20 strokes off / 40 strokes racing, 20 strokes off

6 × 30sec racing with 15 seconds off / 60 seconds racing with 30 seconds off / 90 seconds racing with 45 seconds off

6 × 500m racing with 2 minutes off

Alactic training

4 × (4 × 8 strokes on, 20 strokes off) at race rate or faster

4 × (4 × 12 strokes on, 20 strokes off) at race rate or faster

1 stroke racing, 1 stroke dead light / 2 strokes racing, 2 strokes dead light / 3 strokes racing, 3 strokes dead light – build up to 12 strokes racing with 12 strokes dead light in between

12 × (12 strokes half-slide building speed sets with 12 strokes dead light in between)

12 × (12 strokes racing sets with 6 strokes dead light in between)

Combination sessions

Depending on the amount of time that rowers have for training in the week, it is possible to combine sessions from the various training zones so that the rower gets the appropriate training stimulus. These sessions should start and finish with steady state and build in intensity.

Rowing Training

100-minute session

30 minutes steady state at a stroke rate 18–20

15 minutes at stroke rate 24

8 minutes light

10 minutes at stroke rate 28

7 minutes light

2 × 5min at stroke rate 32 with 5 minutes off

15 minutes steady state

60-minute session

20 minutes steady state at a stroke rate 18–20

3 × 5min flat stroke rates 28/30/32 with 5 minutes light

15 minutes steady state

60-minute session

20 minutes steady state at stroke rates 18–20 with 6 × (12 stroke sprints with 6 strokes off)

3 × 4min at flat stroke rates in each piece at 30/32/34 with 4 minutes off

20 minutes steady state at rate 18–20 with 6 × (12 stroke sprints with 6 strokes off)

Environment

Variation in training needs to be considered in terms of making the most of your training environment. Rowing clubs and programmes are run on rivers, lakes, canals, marinas and bays. The water can be tidal, have stream or recreational or commercial shipping traffic and be of varying rowable length. It is important to make your environment work for you. Setting up distance markers and timing sessions to get the best quality water and supplementing your water work with land training can improve the quality of training a rower gets. Many successful rowers have come from clubs where there is limited water; they have developed technical skills on the water but have developed aerobically through ergometer, running and cycling training.

Gearing and rigging

Gearing in rowing refers to the manipulation of the levers used in the rowing system to 'load' the rower during the stroke. When racing, if the boat is geared too hard (a heavy gearing) the crew will come out of the start too fast due to overworking their stroke, and fall away with their speed later on in the race. Conversely, if a crew is geared too lightly (an easy gearing) they will demonstrate a very high cadence without creating speed through distance per stroke, and will be passed by crews who have a more effective power application.

Rigging applies to the boat set-up and the adjustments needed to make the rower effective and comfortable. This can consist of height adjustments of the gate on the rigger, changes to seat and feet height, as well as where the rower's foot-stretcher is placed in the boat's cockpit.

We will focus first on the role of the boat's gearing and how it can be adjusted to assist a rower's training and speed development. Gearing can also be adjusted to better prepare crews for racing in strong wind conditions. Easing the gearing in strong head wind conditions and tightening it in a strong tail wind can ensure that the crew is not overloaded in the slower head wind or over-rated and underpowered in the fast tail wind.

The key is to find the right balance in the gearing that is specific to the rowers in the crew. There are some standard general rigging parameters that are always good to use as a starting point; however, the individuals and what they bring to the boat need to be considered when rigging and gearing a boat.

There are some terms that you will need to know in order to understand how best to use rigging and gearing as a training aid. As gearing relates to the rower's and crew's levers, adjustments to the rigger and gate as well as the oar will determine the boat's gearing. The term 'spread' is used in sweep rowing and is

41

Rowing Training

Boat type	Span/Spread (cm)	Scull/Oar Length (cm)	Inboard (cm)
Single Scull	159–160	288–290	88–89
Double Scull	158–160	289–291	87–88
Quad Scull	158–160	289–292	87–89
Coxless Pair	85–86	376–377	116–117
Coxed Pair	86–87	375–376	115–116
Coxless Four	84–86	375–377	114–116
Coxed Four	85–86	375–377	115–116
Eight	83–84	375–377	113–114

Fig. 3.1: Standard rigging ranges for men.

Boat type	Span/Spread (cm)	Scull/Oar Length (cm)	Inboard (cm)
Single Scull	159–161	287–289	87–89
Double Scull	159–160	287–290	87–89
Quad Scull	158–160	288–290	87–88
Coxless Pair	86–87	372–373	116–117
Coxless Four	84–85	372–374	114–115
Eight	83–84	373–375	113–114

Fig. 3.2: Standard rigging ranges for women.

the distance from the centre line of the boat (keel) to the centre of the rigger pin. As there are two riggers for each rower in a sculling boat the term 'span' is used, being the measurement from the centre of the rigger pin on the starboard side to the centre of the rigger pin on the port side. The 'oar or scull length' is the overall length of the oar or scull measured down its loom (shaft) from the tip of the blade to the end of the handle. The 'inboard' is measured from the end of the handle to the outboard side of the oar's or scull's collar. The 'outboard' is the measurement from the outboard side of the collar to the tip of the blade measured along the middle of the oar's or scull's loom.

For your reference, Figs. 3.1 and 3.2 are tables of standard rigging ranges. The aim is to give you a sense of the range and for you to experiment with and find what works best for your crew.

Gearing ratios

In order to compare rigs that are geared differently, a simple calculation can be done to produce a gearing ratio. There are different equations for sculling and sweep boats and it is meant to be a practical solution for comparison. Ideally the length of the oar's or scull's outboard is used from the outboard side of the loom's collar to the centre of blade pressure. There is a variety of blade shapes and sizes available, so for consistency a hypothetical centre of pressure at 12 centimetres is used for both sculling and sweep equations.

Sculling

$$\frac{\text{Length of scull (minus inboard) (minus 12)}}{\text{Half the scull's span}}$$

If a single scull is rigged with a span of 159cm, overall scull length of 289cm and an inboard of 88cm, the equation will be:

$$\frac{289-88-12}{79.5} = \frac{189}{79.5} = \text{a gearing ratio of } 2.377$$

If we compare this rig with a single scull with a span of 160cm, overall scull length of 288cm and an inboard of 88cm where the gearing ratio is 2.350, we can see that this ratio is less and therefore lighter in gearing than the heavier rig with a 2.377 ratio.

Sweep

$$\frac{\text{Length of oar (minus inboard) (minus 12)}}{\text{Spread}}$$

If a coxless pair has a spread of 87cm, oar length of 377cm and an inboard of 117cm the gearing ratio equation is:

$$\frac{377-117-12}{87} = \frac{248}{87} = \text{a gearing ratio of } 2.850$$

Again, comparing this rig with another coxless pair with a spread of 86cm, oar length of 377cm and an inboard of 116cm that has a gearing ratio of 2.895, we can see that with a shorter spread and inboard the rig is harder than the rig with a 2.850 ratio.

These ratios show how the load can be changed through manipulation of the boat's sculls, oars and riggers. Bringing the rower's foot-stretcher towards the stern so that his forward arc is more acute at the catch will also provide more load due to a more ineffective placement position at the catch; conversely, bringing the foot-stretcher back towards the bow of the boat will lighten the load.

Spoon shapes also provide a way to manipulate the loading of a rower. The larger the surface area of the blade shape, the greater the loading.

On the practical side, changing outboard length to increase or decrease a rower's gearing has a large effect and is easier to change than re-rigging the span or spread of the boat's riggers.

Rowing biomechanists Valery Kleshnev and Volke Nolte carried out some research into differing oar lengths (Rowing Biomechanics Newsletter, www.biorow.com, September 2011). They concluded that the main differences between hard- and light-geared boats lie in blade efficiency with the lighter gearing, because the rower has to spend more energy moving water at the blade. This makes for a faster drive phase in the lighter gearing than the harder gearing. The rower's forces, power and boat speed are not significantly altered. Their advice to coaches is that they should not be shy in experimenting with big changes in a rower's outboard oar length.

As you can see, the rationale is there to use changes in gearing to manipulate the speed of the drive phase of the stroke. This has potential for training and speed development. The boat can be 'geared up' through increasing the oar's or scull's outboard or adding extra drag on the boat's hull (through wrapping a bungee around the hull or adding a sea anchor) and therefore increasing the drive time of the drive phase of the stroke. This is very good for rowing-specific in-boat strength and power training. There are a number of training patterns

Rowing Training

that can be used, including low stroke rates (12–16 strokes a minute) for sets of 20 to 30 strokes. Longer 2,000m low to mid-rate pieces (18–26 strokes per minute) with resistance build rowing power and can help emphasize rhythm. Geared-up racing starts and racing pieces allow maximum power and effort to be applied over a longer drive phase; when the gearing is lightened and the drag on the hull back to normal the contrast is extreme for the rower, and he is now able to work on applying all the power he has been delivering at a faster rate and boat speed.

With a lighter gearing (decreasing the oar's or scull's outboard) it is possible to do rowing-specific neural, rhythm and pacing training. The faster drive phase means that the rower has to move more quickly to read the boat at the changes of direction at the catch and finish and apply his power. This means that the rower can practise keeping the boat moving at a consistent speed and rhythm without overworking the boat.

Steady state training with a lighter gearing provides a technical advantage as the rower's drive time is closer to his racing drive time but without the physiological cost. Sprint training done with the lighter gearing and the speed it brings to the drive phase helps the athleticism and neural training of the rower. Measured time pieces over set distances (500 to 2,000m) and set rates (24–34 strokes per minute) allow the rower to keep the boat up and moving in a similar way to that of the middle of a race.

Through trial and error, imaginative rowers and coaches can reap rewards and be ahead of the competition by finding out what rig works for them in training, different weather conditions and racing.

Crew

Learning to row different boat types helps the rower progress from a rower to an oarsman. Single and double sculls as well as pairs offer the greatest learning for a rower as he can feel the effects of what he is doing on the boat and how the boat is responding. Small boats also offer a very competitive situation in training: as the saying goes, the best coach is the boat that is sitting off your stern. In small boats there is also the opportunity for more specialization and individualization of the training programme. Practicalities, resources and the type of programme may mean that your club has predominantly big boats: quads, fours and eights. These too can work well, but in a different way. Learning to apply power more quickly to move with the faster boats and the added teamwork required all add to the allure of these boat classes. Ideally, a rower will experience both small and big boat rowing in his programme, to develop him technically, mentally and increase his physicality.

Coaching

There are many ways for a rower to receive feedback on how he is rowing and moving with the boat and his crew. Often it is a coach who is pulling together the programme, providing the technical model, pastoral care and direction for the rower and crew. How much coaching is too much? How much isn't enough? Do you need a coach every session or every stroke?

What works best is an individual thing. Generally, behind every great crew there is a great coach. Conversely, behind every great coach is a great bunch of talented rowers. It is still the rower doing the rowing and his ownership, responsibility and desire to change, share and push on is fundamental to getting the most out of the knowledge and enthusiasm of his coach. The real understanding of how the boat moves and how to time the drive together comes to the rower through self-discovery as well as from his crewmates. Mixing up rowers of varying ability provides good challenges both for the newer rowers to step up and for the experienced rowers to have to think through and articulate to the newer rowers how to move the boat, train, pace a race and compete. This process, along with an astute coaching eye, results in a powerful feedback combination.

Training aids

Along with the technical and coaching feedback, there are now a lot of products available to help the rower and coach understand the crew's performance. While the coach's best aid is still his stopwatch and the rower's his speed coach, there are now biomechanical systems commercially available that can feed back to the coach and rower the boat's acceleration and velocity traces, stroke length and stroke power, as well as force curves and power synchronicity. There are apps and products that connect these parameters 'live' between the rower and the coach. There are apps that use sound to connect the rower with the boat's acceleration, and apps where music has been composed to assist in the rower's rhythm development. Detailed video analysis has also become part of a rower and coach's tool bag now that technology has moved so quickly and these tools have become affordable. While all these products are very useful, it is important for the rower and coach to prioritize feedback and work on the basics.

CHAPTER 4

ERGOMETER TRAINING

Increasing numbers of rowing machines of increasing variety are coming onto the market. There are machines with fixed heads, fixed seats, moving heads and seats; ergometers that use either air or water for a brake; ergometers on sliders; for sculling; for sweep; and those that join together and can be rowed like a crew. There are instrumented ergometers and ergometers that provide detailed analysis of each workout.

Ergometers are a very useful tool in a rower's toolbox; also, indoor rowing is increasing in popularity in gyms around the world. There are championship events, world records across different age groups and marathon ergometer events that are popular ways to raise money for charities and appeals.

Different ergometers give a different 'feel' and different learning points. Most have adjustable settings and the 'drag' or resistance can either be lightened or made harder. Adjusting the drag during workouts is a good way to challenge the rower both technically and physically. With a very high drag the rower feels he is working very hard against a big load. This is great if you are doing power strokes and are looking for maximal work done. This type of load will keep the rate low and you will need to keep an eye on the length of the stroke to ensure it is not shortening.

Conversely, a very light setting will mean the rower will have to apply his power very quickly to keep up with the speed of the fan. Rowers should experiment with the drag factors they use in ergometer races and training and find the one that works best for them.

Not only are ergometers an effective physiological training tool, they can also be used to help the rower understand and develop his technique. Ergometers on sliders and with moving heads and/or seats enable the rower to work on the timing between his hands connecting the head and the power he applies through his legs.

The most effective part of the rowing machine is the instant feedback that the rower is getting stroke by stroke. His stroke rate, time, watts (power), split (time per 500m) and force curve are all there for him to see and use.

There is no hiding place on an ergometer and it is an individual performance, therefore it is an ideal testing and training tool and modality. On the water, varying weather and water conditions as well as the influence of other crew members make it hard to judge and monitor the contribution and work of an individual rower. Having ergometer training as part of the rower's programme allows for his true physiological development to be tracked and his training to be monitored.

As indoor rowing develops its own identity and momentum, gym users and classes are becoming more elaborate with their training and the different uses of the ergometer. Whether on the water or on land, balance and variation in training will give the rower the best chance of improvement.

Ergometer Training

Ergometer training sessions

Below is a selection of ergometer workloads for the various physiological training zones.

Strength and power sessions

10 × 10 strokes maximal force strokes at rate 12–14 strokes per minute with 30 strokes off × 4 with 3 minutes off in between sets

10 × 10 strokes maximal force at strokes at rates 14/16/18/20 strokes per minute with 30 strokes off × 4 and 3 minutes off in between sets

8 × 20 strokes at maximal power at stroke rates 14/16/18/20 × 4 with 30 strokes off and 2 minutes off in between sets

8 × 20 strokes at maximal power at stroke rates 14/18/22/26 × 4 with 30 strokes off and 2 minutes off in between sets

8 × 20 strokes at maximal power at stroke rates 22/26/30/34 × 4 with 30 strokes off and 2 minutes off in between sets

Relay power race: teams of 4–5 rowers take 10 maximal power strokes each until they reach 2,000m (or another prescribed distance). First team to 2,000m wins. Rowers will need to work out how to get on and off the ergometer quickly and straight into the power strokes. While a rower is on the machine rowing, another is holding his feet, another holding the ergometer head and another is ready to get on. They then rotate through their positions.

Lactate tolerance

3 × 5 × 1min at stroke rates 20/24/28/32 with 75 seconds off in between pieces and 5 minutes between sets

3 × 5 × 1min at stroke rates 24/28/32/36 with 75 seconds off in between pieces and 5 minutes between sets

2 × 10 × 30sec on, 45 seconds off, at stroke rates 24/26/28/32/36 with 5 minutes off between sets

2 × 10 × 30sec on, 45 seconds off, at stroke rates 28/32/36/>36 with 5 minutes off between sets

Transport

4 × 1,500m with 1,000m at stroke rate 26 and the last 500m at free rate with 5 minutes off. Another variation is to row 1,000m at the rower's target 2,000m split plus 5 seconds for 1,000 metres then pull the split down to the target 2,000m split.

4 × 1,500m, at flat stroke rates 26/28/30/32 with 5 minutes off in between sets

4 × 1,500m: 2 × with stroke rate changes at each 500m of 26/28/30, and 2 × with stroke rate changes at each 500m of 30/32/34

4 × 5min on, 5 minutes off at set stroke rates 26/28/30/32

Anaerobic threshold

4 × 2,000m at flat stroke rates: 2 × 2,000m at stroke rates 24 and 26, and 2 × 2,000m at stroke rates 26 and 28, with 6–10 minutes off in between pieces

4 × 2,000m with rate steps at the 1,000m mark: 2 × 2,000m at stroke rates 24/26, and 2 × 2,000m at stroke rates 26/28, with 6–10 minutes off in between pieces

4 × 2,000m with rate changes at 500m and 1,500m (500m/1,000m/500m): 2 × 2,000m at stroke rates 26/24/26, and 2 × 2,000m at stroke rates 28/26/28, with 6–10 minutes off in between pieces

3 × 15min at 5-minute changes and flat rates: 1 × 5min stroke rate changes at stroke rate 24/26/28, 1 × flat stroke rate at stroke rate 26, 1 × 5min stroke rate changes at stroke rate 26, 1 × 5min stroke rate changes at stroke rate

Ergometer Training

28/26/28, with 8–12 minutes off in between pieces

3 × 20min with flat stroke rates at stroke rates 22, 24 and 22, with 8–15 minutes off in between pieces

3 × 20min with stroke rate changes at 10 minutes: 1 × 20min with stroke rate changes at 10 minutes at stroke rates 22/24, 1 × 20min with stroke rate changes at 10 minutes at stroke rates 23/25, 1 × 20min with stroke rate changes at 10 minutes at stroke rates 24/26, with 8–15 minutes off in between pieces

Steady state aerobic training

Ergometer training provides an excellent vehicle for steady state training – anywhere from 12 to 20 kilometres of continuous rowing at a stroke rate between 18 and 20 strokes a minute. A good practice is to have a very short break every 30 minutes to stretch the rower's back and rehydrate.

2,000m ergometer competitions

The most popular ergometer test is the speed at which a rower can complete a 2,000m piece on the rowing machine.

The indoor test has different characteristics from the water. Firstly, there is no external focus or race demand, no crew to attack or push away from – it is man (or woman) and machine. Secondly, there is immediate feedback on how hard the rower is working every stroke.

Pacing is a lot easier to achieve and physiologically an evenly paced race using a greater aerobic contribution will produce a better score. As a rule of thumb the rower should be approximately 2 seconds quicker in his first 500m than he is in his average split over the whole 2,000m. Once he is over 4 seconds, the last 500m can be a pretty catastrophic affair.

That is not to say that the rower should not go out hard – just not too hard.

There is no escaping that the 2,000m test will be brutal, painful and exhausting. The rower will need to confront it and aggressively go out after his personal best. He has to prepare well mentally.

Preparation and confidence are key ingredients to achieving a good 2,000m score. The rower's ergometer preparation needs to provide him with the confidence to pull the split he needs. Regular ergometer sessions of varying intensity allow the rower to explore his pacing and his limits. He needs to arrive on race day knowing he is in shape and has got enough work behind him to be sure that his execution of the test will give him the score he is looking for.

He needs to go to the test trusting his preparation and believing he can pull the split he needs. He also needs to be ambitious with his scores and take a risk to explore his limits, all in a rhythm and pacing it well.

Regular ergometer sessions during the rower's training will allow him to develop his aspirations and goals as well as his confidence on the ergometer. A lot of variety can be had in training on the ergometer.

Ten to twelve weeks out from the ergometer race or test, the rower's training could include a variety of longer distance ergometer sessions so that he gets to hone his rhythm and power. An understanding of the relationship between the rower's power and rate is also important. Steady state aerobic ergometer sessions allow for this and set a good base level of power per stroke that he can build upon.

Over-distance ergometer pieces at 5,000m, 6,000m and/or 20 or 30 minutes are also very good preparation for a 2,000m test. These can be fixed rate, step rates or open rates, such as the sample sessions previously described in this chapter. These pieces will be where the rower can develop his anaerobic threshold

Ergometer Training

power and rhythm. As they are long enough to challenge his physiology, they give him a good sense of pacing for the 2,000m. Only using short pieces for ergometer preparation can give an overly optimistic prediction of where the rower's 2,000m score may be, and the splits he sets as a result may be over-ambitious.

Sample 2,000m performance preparation pieces

2,000m pieces with stroke rate changes at 500m and 1,500m (500m/1,000m/500m) allow the rower to practise his 2,000m ergometer race profile. He can prepare for the toughness of the third 500m with flat splits and build in the last 500m. Stroke rates can be individualized and be built through the preparation stages at 28/26/28, 30/28/30 and 32/30/32.

A series of 250m or 500m with a similar length off at the rower's target 2,000m pace builds feel, rhythm and confidence at the target pace. There needs to be enough pieces that the rower can handle the first few relatively easily then has to work hard but achieves the last few.

3–4 × 750m pieces coming off the start and on to the rower's 2,000m ergometer race pace and rhythm will build his confidence and ability to start and come on to the correct pace to set him up for the next 1,250m.

On race or test day the rower should be confident in his preparation and stick to his race plan and race day rituals. It's a great opportunity to explore his physiology and psychology.

The ergometer manufacturer Concept 2 from the USA publishes a series of world records over the following distances: 500m, 1,000m, 2,000m, 5,000m, 6,000m, 10,000m, 21,097m, 42,195m, 30 minutes and 60 minutes.

Figs 4.1 to 4.4 show the current world record times for 2,000m on the Concept 2 ergometer. All age groups are listed: lightweight weights are at or below 61.5kg for women and 75kg for men. Heavyweight is an open division above these weights. As you can see from the age range of these records, indoor rowing competitions are for all.

Age Category	Name	Country	Record	Season
13–18	Karsten Brodowsky	GER	05:47.0	2004
19–29	Rob Waddell	NZL	05:38.3	1999
30–39	Rob Waddell	NZL	05:36.6	2008
40–49	Paved Shurmen	BLR	05:47.8	2017
50–54	Andy Ripley	GBR	06:07.7	1998
55–59	Thomas Darling	USA	06:12.6	2014
60–64	Paul Hendershott	USA	06:23.7	2004
65–69	Chris Cooper	USA	06:39.5	2017
70–74	Roger Borggaard	USA	06:52.1	2016
75–79	Paul Guest	AUS	07:13.2	2015

Figure 4.1 Heavyweight men (75 kilograms plus), 2,000m World Records from Concept 2.

Ergometer Training

Figure 4.1 continued

Age Category	Name	Country	Record	Season
80–84	Carlo Zezza	USA	07:34.4	2017
85–89	Dean Smith	USA	08:10.5	2013
90–94	Robert Spenger	USA	08:42.4	2011
95–99	Stephen Richardson	USA	13:21.5	2016

Fig. 4.1: continued

Age Category	Name	Country	Record	Season
13–18	Henrik Stephansen	DEN	06:06.5	2007
19–29	Henrik Stephansen	DEN	05:56.7	2013
30–39	Eskild Ebbesen	DEN	06:06.4	2004
40–49	Jesus Gonzalez	ESP	06:14.9	2016
50–54	Paul Siebach	USA	06:25.1	2009
55–59	Roy Brook	GBR	06:38.1	2006
60–64	Brian Bailey	GBR	06:42.5	2007
65–69	Tor Arne Simonsen	Nor	06:51.7	2016
70–74	Arnold Cooke	GBR	07:08.2	2011
75–79	Roger Bangay	GBR	07:24.1	2012
80–84	Geoffery Knight	GBR	07:40.4	2015
85–89	Robert Spenger	USA	08:13.6	2010
90–94	Robert Spenger	USA	8:44.9	2015
95–99	John Hodgson	GBR	10:28.2	2006
100+	John Hodgson	GBR	13:32.6	2011

Fig. 4.2: Lightweight men (75 kilograms or less), 2,000m World Records from Concept 2.

Age Category	Name	Country	Record	Season
>12	Fie Udby	DEN	07:30.3	1998
13–18	Sofia Asoumanaki	GRE	06:28.2	2016
19–29	Olena Buryak	UKR	06:25.0	2015

Figure 4.3 Heavyweight women (61.5 kilograms plus), 2000m World Records from Concept 2.

Ergometer Training

Figure 4.3 continued

Age Category	Name	Country	Record	Season
30–39	Sarah Winckless	GBR	06:28.8	2004
40–49	Carol Skricki	USA	06:48.2	2003
50–54	Joanne Ritchie	CAN	06:58.0	2012
55–59	Anne Bourlioux	CAN	07:10.1	2016
60–64	Mies Bernelot–Moens	NED	07:31.1	2008
65–69	Mies Bernelot Moeis	NED	07:43.2	2011
70–74	Mies Bernelot Moeis	NED	08:00.8	2016
75–79	Luanne Mills	USA	08:29.6	2015
80–84	Ruth Doell	USA	08:54.8	2008
85–89	Sally Callahan	USA	10:34.7	2015

Fig. 4.3: continued

Age Category	Name	Country	Record	Season
13–18	Christine Cavallo	USA	07:05.7	2013
19–29	Ursula Grobler	USA	06:54.7	2010
30–39	Lisa Schlenker	USA	06:56.7	2000
40–49	Lisa Schlenker	USA	07:09.6	2005
50–54	Joan Van Blom	USA	07:22.6	2004
55–59	Joan Van Blom	USA	07:30.6	2008
60–64	Susan Hooten	USA	07:35.5	2015
65–69	Ingrid Petersen	DEN	07:56.7	2012
70–74	Luanne Mills	USA	08:12.7	2009
75–79	Luanne Mills	USA	08:34.7	2014
80–84	Jeanne Daprano	GBR	09:28.3	2017
85–89	Jane Welsh	GBR	10:25.2	2006
90–94	Ernestine Bayer	USA	12:07.5	2000
95–99	Dorothy Stewart	USA	14:55.3	2017

Fig. 4.4: Lightweight women (61.5 kilograms or less), 2000m World Records from Concept 2.

CHAPTER 5

SPECIFIC ROWING CONDITIONING

In specific rowing conditioning there should ideally be a sequential progression from flexibility to strength then endurance. This means that the rower is flexible enough to get into the rowing positions, strong enough to hold them, then has enough local and global muscle endurance to maintain them. In practice there is rarely enough time to develop each component sequentially, so the rower's programme becomes concurrent. The coach and rower should consider what the individual's needs are and prioritize them within the programme accordingly. Specific rowing conditioning also allows the rower to acquire a greater understanding of how his body moves, engages and relaxes during the rowing stroke: how his global whole-body strength might be high, but his local and specific strength might be low. This situation can see a rower put a lot of work in through his legs and shoulders but miss the vital connection and strength through his trunk, resulting in a less effective drive phase and power application.

Specific rowing endurance

As the overload principle applies to specific strength conditioning, so it applies to endurance. The exercises below can be incorporated into the rower's circuit work. The progression can be built for each exercise from 30-second intervals out to 2–3 minutes. When doing this type of conditioning it is vital that the rower holds his form. Once fatigue or loss of concentration moves the rower from holding the correct positioning with correct muscle engagement, he should stop and reset. Generally at this point the rower's global strength and endurance has taken over from his local strength and endurance.

Specific fitness circuits for rowing

Circuit design

Specific circuit work for rowers has a place in every rower's programme. Along with the rowing machine, circuit work provides an effective land-based training tool to both supplement and enhance the rower's on-water work and fitness. When devising a circuit, consideration needs to be taken of the training age and physical development of the rower, the programme goals and the equipment available. A specific rowing circuit should contain elements of leg-based exercises, pulling exercises, pushing exercises and trunk work. Popular leg-based exercises include front and back squats, single-legged squats and leg press, bench pulls with either an Olympic bar or dumbbells, and bench press with either the Olympic bar or dumbbells. Trunk work should see a lot of sit-up variations as well as back extensions. For the advanced athlete, power cleans offer a whole body exercise that is closest to the rowing movement, with the legs and trunk working together.

Specific Rowing Conditioning

Balance
When putting your circuit together always consider using exercises that provide balance to the rower's conditioning. The way skeletal muscles work is that there is an agonist muscle which causes the muscle movement through its contraction (for example, the arm's biceps when drawing the handle through at the finish of the rowing stroke) and an antagonist muscle, which opposes the agonist, enabling the movement to be controlled and returned (the arm's triceps play this role during the arm draw). In the example above, often by strengthening the triceps the rower's strength in pulling is increased. Therefore, the circuit should address both the agonist and antagonist muscles, using rowing-specific and general physical development exercises.

Agility
Although rowing is a weight-supported repetitive closed-cycle sport, agility and coordination are important. Balancing the boat in a seated position isn't a natural balance position for bipedal humans. Apart from balancing the boat, the rower also needs to have good timing and coordination at the front turn between his hands, feet and the boat to place the oar in the water and apply his power through the foot-stretcher. He needs to instantaneously apply his power to get the boat accelerating quickly in the drive phase. Skipping, box jumps, plyometric exercises and running can all be added to the rower's circuits and programmes to enhance his athleticism and agility.

Free weights vs machine weights
There are pros and cons to both types of resistant tools. Both have a place and often it will depend on what is available in your local gym or club. Free weights offer the advantage of having to use tendons and ligaments to balance and stabilize the body under load in a more open environment, so the rower and his body need to adapt and develop through a greater number of the body's structures in an athletic way. Fixed machine weights, on the other hand, offer a safe and less technically challenging way of lifting. This means that the load can be greater for the training stimulus. When taking the issues into consideration, the rower's technical competence needs to be given some thought. Safe lifting with good technique has to be the first priority, and machine weights offer a safe environment. It is good practice to connect with strength and conditioning expertise to help improve the rower's lifting technique.

Load and repetitions
A circuit can be used to provide a very effective training stimulus to a variety of physiological training zones. Through manipulating the repetitions, load and exercise selection, while monitoring the rower's heart rate and lactate as well as load lifted or time taken to complete a circuit, coaches and rowers can measure progress and understand what training stimulus and adaptation they are achieving from the training.

Mental toughness
Circuits also provide other opportunities to work on mental robustness and resilience during a physical challenge. They can put the rower into an uncomfortable place that he is not certain to pull out of. Like in a race, the rower needs to stay in his rhythm, hold form and push on.

Specific Rowing Conditioning

No. of Exercises	Duration	Cadence Guide	Repetition and Sets	Loading	Central Physiological Marker – Lactate Accumulation	Physiological Load
15	2 minutes	20 per minute	30min × 2–3 (continuous)	Low load high reps	1–3 mmol	Aerobic
9	90 seconds each	24	10–15min × 4–5 (90sec between sets)	Low load high reps	2–3 mmol	Aerobic
7	90 seconds each	28	11min × 4–5	Medium load medium reps	3–5 mmol	Anaerobic threshold
7	60 seconds each	34	7min × 4–6	High load medium reps	5–9 mmol	Transport

Fig. 5.1: Rowing circuit training matrix.

Specific Rowing Conditioning

Sample exercises

Whole body
Power cleans
    Dumbbell cleans
    High pulls
    Dead lifts
    Power strokes on an ergometer
    Good mornings
    Weighted standing swings
    Seated cable row
    Snatch
    Skipping

Lower body
    Back squats
    Front squats
    Leg press
    One-legged squats
    Weighted step-ups
    Squat jumps
    Lunges
    Hamstring curls
    Legs-only ergometer
    Running

Upper body
    Bench pull
    Dumbbell bench pull
    Bench press
    Dumbbell bench press
    Lat pull-downs
    Chin-ups
    Overhead press
    Bent-over rows
    Push-ups
    Single arm row

Trunk
    Abdominal curls
    Lateral abdominal curls
    Back extension
    Reverse curls
    Plank
    Static ergometer hold
    Good mornings
    Medicine ball sit-ups
    Medicine ball with partner throws
    Weighted thoracic twists

CHAPTER 6

STRENGTH TRAINING

Strength training

Strength training has been part of rowing training programmes for many years. However, it is important to recognize the rationale for its inclusion in relation to rowing performance. Around 70 per cent of the total muscle mass of a rower is used to accelerate the boat. Around 46 per cent of the leg muscle, 31 per cent of the trunk and 23 per cent of the arm muscle contributes to the rowing stroke. The legs utilize 95 per cent of their maximum capacity, the trunk 55 per cent and the arms 75 per cent. Rowing is a whole body activity, requiring excellent coordination from the legs to the arms. Research has shown that peak force in the first ten strokes of a 2,000m race is estimated to be 1,352N (Newtons) (around 135kg) for males, and 1,019N (101kg) for females. Male single scullers can produce anywhere between 1,000 and 1,500N during the first 10 seconds of racing. This is primarily because the boat is starting from a stationary position. The average force a rower produces for the remainder of the race is between 65 and 70 per cent of the maximum of that rower. When measuring power on the oar handle, values of 450–550 watts have been seen. Power produced during five power strokes on the ergometer has been used to predict rowing performance, along with several other endurance performance markers.

Rowers who have greater force and power capability can improve their economy. Therefore, stronger athletes are more economical by having a greater fatigue resistance and a better anaerobic capacity when compared to athletes who are less strong. These are desirable physical qualities for successful rowers, as for the same given workload the metabolic demand will be less.

With the lightweight rowing class being weight restricted, racing is more competitive, with smaller margins of victory. For instance, in the final of the lightweight men's double at the Rio 2016 Olympics, the time margin between first and third was 0.69 seconds, with Ireland beating Norway by 0.16 seconds and losing to France by 0.53 seconds. Racing margins are generally smaller than the openweight category. This requires crews to be very technically proficient and physically robust for their body mass. A slight deficit in either can cost a rower a medal or even a place in a final. The optimization of power to body mass ratio is as critical to racing as a technical component for lightweight rowers.

Rowers must have a carefully planned mix of both aerobic and anaerobic physical qualities. Both have been demonstrated to have an impact on rowing performance. The use of more anaerobic-type training, including strength training, is important to the development of peak power and force production, which has been shown to be critical for rowing performance. This presents a unique challenge compared to events of a similar duration, such as 5,000m track racing, as the training for rowers needs to have some considerable time devoted to the anaerobic component of

Strength Training

	Monday	**Tuesday**	**Wednesday**	**Thursday**	**Friday**	**Saturday**	**Sunday**
Session 1	Off	12km Ergo	16km Rate 24	16km Rate 24	12km Ergo	20km Rate 18/19	30 minute Ergo Rate 20
Session 2	Off	Weights	12km Ergo	Weights	Off	12km inc. 2 × 4000m Rate 22	Weights

Fig 6.1: Typical training week for a high performance club rower.

strength training to develop these force and power characteristics.

During a rower's training week, there is a heavy emphasis on endurance-type training with anywhere between one and four strength training sessions to be expected throughout the week. Trying to accomplish both endurance and strength training simultaneously is a significant challenge, as endurance training can compromise training adaptation from strength training. This is because both types of training are attempting to physiologically change different components of the muscular-skeletal system and biological systems. The same cannot be said for the impact of strength training on endurance training. In fact, strength training has been shown to improve endurance performance.

Several suggestions have been put forward to explain why strength training is compromised with the introduction of endurance training. When there is a large volume of endurance training, this can create a large residual fatigue, which carries over into the strength training session. This can result in the rower being unable to lift the same load when compared to a non-fatigued state. Multiple training sessions over a short period of time can also deplete energy stores (glycogen). With less energy, the body is unable to tolerate the next training session, whether that be on the same day or the following day. This can impact on endurance training as much as it does strength training. With large amounts of endurance training the body can shift into a catabolic (breakdown) state, which can temporarily reduce the adaptation that session is trying to achieve.

While a rower may experience a catabolic training effect that may disrupt the subsequent training session, it is the repeated exposure through training that creates the necessary adaptation for rowers. If the rower continues to maintain his body in a catabolic state, the chronic adaptation necessary for physiological changes will be blunted.

In an elite rower's training programme strength training can form up to 20–30 per cent of an adult's weekly training. With such little time during the week dedicated to it, strength training is most likely to be compromised if appropriate programming is not adhered to. Every strength training session must be optimized to overcome the endurance training bias of the week.

Strength training philosophy

The role of strength training is to optimize the rower's force, power and velocity capabilities. Becoming stronger is a nice side effect. There are two primary reasons to develop force. The first is to develop a robust rower. This allows a rower to build a tolerance to high force and velocity loading, reducing risk of injury by enabling him to tolerate repeated loading through the training programme. The second is to improve rower performance by optimizing high force power and velocity capabilities, which are necessary for the sport itself.

Strength Training

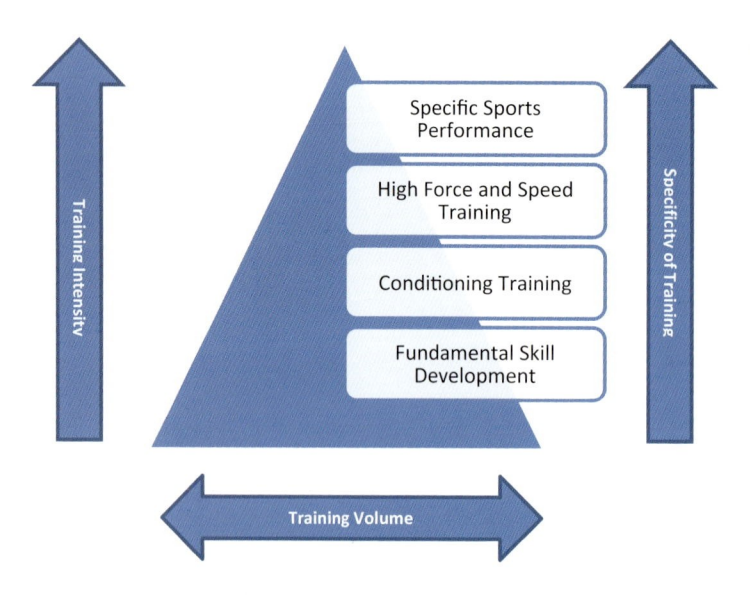

Fig. 6.2: Pyramid of training.

[Pyramid diagram with levels from bottom to top: Fundamental Skill Development, Conditioning Training, High Force and Speed Training, Specific Sports Performance. Left axis: Training Intensity (increasing upward). Right axis: Specificity of Training (increasing upward). Bottom axis: Training Volume.]

The training paradigm in Fig. 6.2 describes a hierarchical model of the amount of volume/time spent on each strength training component. Fundamental skill development is the basis and foundation of physical preparation. Developing excellent skills is critical to enable building of the physical qualities further up the training paradigm. The largest amount of volume is spent in this area, especially with younger rowers. It is the furthest away from specificity of training for rowing, and is the lowest in intensity of all the blocks.

Conditioning training sits above skill development but utilizes these fundamental skills to develop a robust rower, for example, by challenging the rower's tolerance to maintain a movement quality while under stress. It allows him to be exposed to repeated submaximal loading, which builds a greater tolerance to higher loading in the future. This can account for a fairly high volume of training, but with variable intensity; therefore, if intensity increases, volume needs to decrease. This type of training provides the rower with the ability to train regularly and can be termed 'trainability'.

High force and speed training is the third block. The primary objective is to develop the basic physical qualities necessary to row. All sports require force and velocity components, so this is a process of developing those that are fundamental to rowing. There is a lower volume of this work when compared to fundamental skills or conditioning training, and a significantly higher focus on intensity.

The final block of training in this paradigm is specific sports performance. This is racing itself, or training that is close to a racing event. For instance, specific training for a rower may be power strokes or higher rating work on an ergometer or in a boat to develop the power or velocity characteristics seen in rowing. This specific work does not need to be completed in the weight room, but can be completed in the rowing environment.

Heavy strength training

There is significant evidence demonstrating the impact of strength training on force and power development for athletes. The goal of heavy strength training is to increase the rower's ability to generate maximal force. As stated

Strength Training

Loading	Outcome	Load	Speed	Frequency	Sets	Reps	Recovery	Testing
Heavy strength training	Maximal force expression	High	Mod to high	2 to 2 × week	3 to 6 per exercise	1 to 5/6 to 10	3 to 5 mins	Repetition max testing (1RM or predictive 1RM)
Explosive strength training	Power expression and rate of force development (RFD)	Low to mod	Very high	1 to 4 × week	3 to 6 per exercise	1 to 8	3 to 5 mins	Ergo power strokes, countermovement jump (CMJ)
Hypertrophy	Increase in muscle and tendon cross sectional area (CSA)	Mod to high	Mod	3 to 6 × week	4 to 8 per exercise	6 to 25+	1 to 3 mins	Body mass, skinfolds and limb girths
Strength conditioning	Tissue robustness and muscle capacity/tolerance	Low to mod	Low	3 to 6 × week	1 to 10 per exercise	10 to 25+	0 to 3 mins	Trunk, hip and upper body conditioning assessments (e.g. maximum press-ups or single leg calf raises)

Fig. 6.3: Strength training and the associated variables to optimize adaptation.

earlier, becoming stronger from strength training is a nice side effect. Heavy strength training is not undertaken with a time constraint – for instance, a back squat or bench pull with heavy weights will take significantly longer to lift than a jump squat with no weight. Fig. 6.3 outlines the training variables for heavy strength training as well as associated strength training variables that are discussed throughout this chapter.

Muscular strength can be defined as the ability of a muscle or a group of muscles to produce force, with maximal strength being the largest force the musculature can produce. Heavy strength training is the modality to develop maximal strength and therefore improve the rower's ability to produce the large forces necessary for rowing. Heavy strength training can be completed 2–3 times a week with 6–10 sets of multi-joint exercises for adult rowers. Repetitions can be from 1 to 10 per set. The loading needs to be high to very high, therefore the weight must be close to the rower's maximum, taking into consideration his technical competency.

Heavy strength training provides a stimulus for both the muscular architecture (morphology) and neuromuscular system (nervous system control of muscular contractions) to adapt. Morphological adaptations that may be seen include changes in muscle cross-sectional area, muscle fibre length and type. Neuromuscular adaptations may include how many motor units (bundles of muscle fibres activated by a single motor neuron) can be activated, synchronization of motor units and muscular coordination between surrounding muscles. All of these factors will help increase the force application of a muscular contraction. For those with a low strength training history, or those who have not strength trained for several weeks (such as when returning to winter training after the off-season post-competition), the majority of changes in the early stages of strength training will be neuromuscular in nature. This is why a rower may see significant changes in the early part of winter training but find it more difficult to make significant changes later in the season.

It can take anywhere from 6 to 20 weeks to see significant gains through strength training, as will be demonstrated by the actual weight a rower has on the bar. The reasons for variance in time required to develop significant strength gains can be due to training history and experience of lifting, time of the season, the amount of endurance training completed concurrently, and maturation of the athlete. It is important to set realistic goals and expectations when

Strength Training

writing a strength training programme, in that the rower must be provided with enough time to become stronger. It is also important to recognize that the progress made each year will not be the same as the year before, primarily due to the rower making big progress in the early years. Making large percentage gains becomes more difficult as years of heavy strength training are accumulated. However, for elite rowers working in an Olympiad, small year-on-year progressions are essential. A 3–4 per cent change each year could result in an overall change of about 10–15 per cent change over a four-year period. This may be enough to tip the balance in favour of being a very forceful rower by the time the Olympics arrive.

As highlighted above, a single session of strength training will have minimal impact on the rower's ability to generate force. It is the cumulative effect of multiple strength training sessions that develops this. It is important to follow certain guidelines, as a rower who can lift 120kg for 10 repetitions, but only lifts 50kg, gets a very different adaptation than he would by lifting 120kg. Ideally, when heavy strength training, a rower should always attempt to lift at 80 per cent or more of that which he can for the given repetition range. This ensures that the rower is actually heavy strength training, and allows him to cyclically alter his loading so that he does not have to maximally lift every time he goes into the gym. For example, using the same example rower who can squat 120kg for 10 repetitions, he has a 10 repetition maximum (RM). If he lifted 107.5kg for 10 repetitions, that would be 90 per cent of his 10RM. This weight is still heavy enough to ensure appropriate adaptation response from heavy strength training.

Fig. 6.4 highlights what the percentage of a 1RM is when lifting between 1 and 10 repetitions. This demonstrates the typical loading a rower can expect to lift to ensure there is positive strength adaptation from the training programming. Chapter 7 will outline in more detail appropriate strength testing and explain how to use Fig. 6.4 to monitor change within the training programme without having to test a rower's 1RM.

Fig. 6.5 is an example of a four-week heavy strength training programme that is typical within a rowing programme. Note that loads

Repetitions	Percentage of 1RM
1	100%
2	95%
3	93%
4	90%
5	87%
6	85%
7	82%
8	80%
9	77%
10	75%

Fig. 6.4: Repetitions and the expected percentage of a rower's 1RM.

	Week 1 Sets × Reps	% 1RM	Week 2 Sets × Reps	% 1RM	Week 3 Sets × Reps	% 1RM	Week 4 Sets × Reps	% 1RM
Back squat	4 × 8	80%	4 × 6	85%	5 × 5	87%	4 × 3	93%
Leg press	4 × 8	80%	4 × 6	85%	5 × 5	87%	4 × 3	93%
Bench press	4 × 8	80%	4 × 6	85%	5 × 5	87%	4 × 3	93%
Bench pull	4 × 8	80%	4 × 6	85%	5 × 5	87%	4 × 3	93%

Fig. 6.5: Four-week strength training programme.

Strength Training

have not been included, but the expected percentages of load is based on Fig. 6.4.

Explosive strength training

Explosive strength training is the expression of power and is commonly termed power training. Unlike heavy strength training, explosive strength training has a speed component. Power, in simple terms, is force multiplied by velocity. As power is a product of force and velocity, it is possible to train both of these components to improve overall power development. For example, heavy strength training has a larger emphasis on strength and a much lower emphasis on speed. So, while heavy strength training may not be used for power development, power can still be measured.

Explosive strength training can be quickly classified into high load, high velocity exercises through to low load, high velocity exercises. Explosive strength training with a greater emphasis on speed is normally completed with light loading, such as throwing medicine balls. Explosive strength training with an equal emphasis on speed and strength would be typified by Olympic weightlifting, such as a power clean. The power clean has similar requirements for strength and speed. The major focus of explosive strength training, regardless of the load, is producing the maximal velocity of the object being lifted or thrown, or allowing a body segment to move with maximal velocity, such as the arm when throwing a punch.

Explosive strength training can be completed 1–4 times a week, with 6–10 multi-joint exercises per session. As defined above, the loading which is necessary to develop power can be as low as 2–3kg using a medicine ball, to very heavy loads such as a power clean or jump squats. The critical component of explosive strength training is the intention of the rower to move the bar or load as quickly as possible. While a coach may not observe the rower moving quickly, his intent to do so must be present. If the rower does not have the intent to move quickly, the training effect will be minimized. This is particularly true when working with low loads, as the rower is not stressed enough to create the adaptation necessary for power development. Using repetition ranges between 1 and 8 is common; however, as described above, performing 5 repetitions slowly compared with 5 repetitions explosively will result in different adaptations. While there are some morphological adaptations within the musculature (muscle mass increases with heavier loads), the primary adaptation focus from explosive strength training is neuromuscular. This refers to the coordination between the musculature and the nervous system, including the brain. The rate (speed) of contraction as well as the magnitude (how forceful) is important for all sporting actions, as well as the appropriate timing. Creating a training stimulus that challenges the rate and magnitude is critical for explosive strength training, which is why completing an exercise with the intent to move quickly is critical for the success of the appropriate adaptation. Without it, it is not explosive strength training.

Similarly to heavy strength training, explosive strength training can take 4–20 weeks to demonstrate significant differences in power output. However, it is possible to make quick, positive changes in power output with appropriate organization of training. Fig. 6.6 is an example session where explosive strength training is the primary focus. Again, you will notice percentages are listed rather than actual loads. It is important to note that explosive strength training does not have to form a single session within itself and may form part of another session, as outlined in Fig. 6.7, where there is also a heavy strength training focus included. When multiple training focuses are being completed within a session, the one with greater movement or speed or which is more

Strength Training

Exercise	Sets x Reps	% 1RM
Box jumps	4 × 5	Body weight only
Power cleans	4 × 3	90–93%
Loaded jump squats	4 × 5	30–40%
Speed bench pull	4 × 5	30–40%

Fig. 6.6: Explosive strength training programme.

Exercise	Sets x Reps	% 1RM
Power cleans	3 × 3	90–93%
Loaded jump squats	3 × 5	30–40%
Speed bench pull	3 × 5	30–40%
Back squats	4 × 5	87%
Bench pull	4 × 5	87%

Fig. 6.7: Combined explosive strength training with heavy strength training programme.

explosive in nature should be completed first. If heavier, slower strength training is completed first, there is a chance that the residual fatigue will carry across to the explosive strength training exercises and impact the speed of execution, which will also affect the rate of adaptation. This is more evident in less experienced strength-trained athletes; however, even with well trained athletes it is recommended to complete explosive strength training prior to heavy strength training wherever possible.

If you compare the volumes between the programmes in Figs 6.6 and 6.7, whether it is through number of sets or total repetitions completed, they are very similar (16 sets with 72 repetitions and 17 sets with 79 repetitions respectively). This is important, as trying to complete a full explosive strength and heavy strength training programme within the same session would almost double the volume of biological stress on the rower. Not only would the programme take well in excess of 2 hours to complete, but the rower is likely to be negatively overloaded or will self-regulate by reducing the intensity of the lifting to survive the session.

Hypertrophy

The primary objective of hypertrophy training is to increase the cross-sectional area of muscle or tendons. Before embarking on a hypertrophy training programme, it is imperative that the coach of the rower determines that this objective represents the primary goal that he is trying to achieve through this modality, and it should be noted that for the majority of youth and developing rowers hypertrophy training is not necessary.

Traditionally, hypertrophy training has been used as a high-volume element of strength training programmes, but this is not necessarily done with the goal of increasing muscle mass in mind, but rather as a means of improving general fitness. While that type of training is an acceptable modality to include within a rowing programme, it is important to differentiate between the true goal of hypertrophy training and general fitness training. Concurrent training whereby both endurance and strength training are undertaken simultaneously (described in more detail later in this chapter) has a significant impact on strength and hypertrophy gains from training; therefore the ability to significantly increase muscle mass, while not impossible, is difficult to achieve with such a high endurance training volume. If there is a genuine need for a rower to increase muscle mass, appropriate expectations of what is achievable need to be clear from the outset. Typically, a 2–3kg increase in muscle mass can take anything from 10 weeks up to a whole training season. It is important to dedicate the appropriate amount of time and programme organization to allow the rower to attain these muscle mass goals. For instance, due to the interference endurance training has on strength and hypertrophy training, reducing the overall volume of endurance training is essential. Stripping back the amount of endurance training the rower completes to the minimal

Strength Training

level acceptable to continue maintaining or developing endurance performance will allow a much greater opportunity for the rower to increase muscle mass.

Training variables for hypertrophy can be found in Fig. 6.3. Hypertrophy training should be completed anywhere from 3 to 6 times a week, with 6–10 sets of multi-joint exercises. The immediate inclusion of single-joint exercises as a superset (one exercise immediately followed by another without recovery from the first) with the multi-joint, e.g. bench press followed by tricep pull-downs, is an excellent way to ensure the rower has enough training stress to allow for hypertrophy adaptation. The load needs to be moderate to near maximal for the volume of work completed. Repetitions for the multi-joint exercises can be between 6 and 15 repetitions (but can be much higher). The single-joint exercises are typically performed with very high volume repetitions (25+), or to near failure. To increase the work of the muscles, the speed with which the weight is lifted should be under control or even using tempo (e.g. 2 seconds up, 2 seconds down). This avoids the rower using momentum to lift the weight. While it is beyond the scope of this book to discuss in depth nutrition for hypertrophy training, basic guidelines around nutrition can be found in Chapter 11.

While Figs 6.8 and 6.9 outline example hypertrophy training programmes, as discussed above these programmes alone will not be enough to make the significant changes in lean muscle mass. They should be used as a guide on how to complete the training once the entire training week, including the appropriate nutrition, is in place. Each of these are pieces of a jigsaw puzzle and, until all are in place, gains in lean muscle mass will be limited.

You will notice that the programmes in Figs 6.8 and 6.9 have different programming styles, with one having supersetted exercises and the other working with clusters. With regard to the superset programme, the second exercise can either be completed to the prescribed volume or in some cases the coach may prescribe this secondary exercise to failure. This provides an added stress which for some rowers may be necessary to elicit muscle hypertrophy. The cluster programme has a number of repetition windows within a single set. For example, 6 × 10, 8, 5, 3. One set would be completing 10 repetitions, followed by 10 seconds rest, 8 repetitions, 10 seconds rest and so on until reaching 3 repetitions. Reducing recovery between sets for both examples to 90 seconds

	Week 1		Week 2		Week 3		Week 4	
	Sets × Reps	% 1RM	Sets × Reps	% 1RM	Sets × Reps	% 1RM	Sets × Reps	% 1RM
Leg press	4 × 12	> 70%	4 × 15	> 65%	4 × 18	> 60%	4 × 15	> 67%
+ Single leg press*	4 × 12	> 70%	4 × 15	> 65%	4 × 18	> 60%	4 × 15	> 67%
Leg press	4 × 12	> 70%	4 × 15	> 65%	4 × 18	> 60%	4 × 15	> 67%
+ Leg extension*	4 × 12	> 70%	4 × 15	> 65%	4 × 18	> 60%	4 × 15	> 67%
Bench press	4 × 12	> 70%	4 × 15	> 65%	4 × 18	> 60%	4 × 15	> 67%
+ Tricep pull down*	4 × 12	> 70%	4 × 15	> 65%	4 × 18	> 60%	4 × 15	> 67%
Seated row	4 × 12	> 70%	4 × 15	> 65%	4 × 18	> 60%	4 × 15	> 67%
+ Bicep curl*	4 × 12	> 70%	4 × 15	> 65%	4 × 18	> 60%	4 × 15	> 67%

Complete sets to failure to increase mechanical and metabolic stress

Fig. 6.8: Hypertrophy training programme with supersets.

Strength Training

	Week 1		Week 2		Week 3		Week 4	
	Sets × Reps	% 1RM	Sets × Reps	% 1RM	Sets × Reps	% 1RM	Sets × Reps	% 1RM
Leg press	6 × 10,8,5,3	> 70%	6 × 3,5,8,10	> 70%	6 × 5,4,3,2,1	> 80%	6 × 1,2,3,4,5	> 80%
Seated row	6 × 10,8,5,3	> 70%	6 × 3,5,8,10	> 70%	6 × 5,4,3,2,1	> 80%	6 × 1,2,3,4,5	> 80%

Fig. 6.9: Hypertrophy training programme with clusters.

to 2 minutes also ensures the rower is under constant stress, which is needed for muscle hypertrophy. Giving both examples is purposeful as the regular combination of both types of training programmes within the same week seems to be the most effective in stimulating lean muscle mass growth. As stated above, hypertrophy training can be completed up to six times a week, so repeating sessions or having slightly different alterations to the same session is entirely valid and sometimes the most effective way to ensure there is enough stimulus to create the desired adaptation. Sometimes, trying to be more creative and include more variety within the programme can lead to ineffective programmes to reach the training objective. The training objective should always be the primary focus when writing a training programme, not the exercise selection.

Strength condition

The primary objective of strength condition is developing tissue robustness, muscle tolerance and capacity. This is often confused with hypertrophy due to the volume of work; however, the principal goal is not increasing mass but the development of the rower's ability to tolerate repeated submaximal loading (i.e. local muscular endurance and the ability of the rower's soft tissues to withstand training load). If the primary goal is local muscular endurance, training is often organized in a circuit format to continually stress particular body areas. For example, a rower may be asked to complete 10–15 repetitions of lunging followed by 10–15 repetitions of jump squatting. This creates a local muscular endurance around the hips and legs. These are commonly known as specific fitness circuits for rowing, and can be found in more detail in the previous chapter. However, if the goal of strength condition is to improve the soft tissue robustness, much more controlled loading is required. The activity is generally prescribed around areas of high use, such as the trunk, hips, back and shoulders.

The aim of improving tissue robustness is not to develop muscular endurance, but more to do with the quality of the soft tissue in high usage areas of the body. By providing this training stimulus, the body is able to remove old soft tissue, which has a reduced ability to transfer or dissipate forces, and replace it with newer, more striated muscle fibres. These newer muscle fibres are able to more effectively tolerate load and transfer force. There is evidence showing that using frequent low load has the capability of replacing old soft tissue as effectively as high load; however, by having low load exercises the total stress on the rower is significantly reduced and the ability to include it more regularly within the training week is increased. By having regular exposure to this training modality, the rower is able to continue to replace older, less effective (in terms of force production or transfer) soft tissue. For low load training, this can be completed 3–6 times a week for 5–15 minutes. The load is low

Strength Training

Exercise	Focus	Volume
Hip bridge (dumbbell on hips)	Hips	1 x 60 seconds
Dumbbell pullover	Chest wall	1 x 60 seconds
Single arm dumbbell press – left	Chest wall	1 x 60 seconds
Single arm dumbbell press – right	Chest wall	1 x 60 seconds
Dumbbell bentover row	Lumbar spine	1 x 60 seconds
Dumbbell stiff leg deadlift	Lumbar spine	1 x 60 seconds
Split squat – left	Hips	1 x 60 seconds
Split squat – right	Hips	1 x 60 seconds

Fig. 6.10: Strength condition training programme focusing on hips, lumbar spine and chest wall.

to moderate, under a controlled tempo (e.g. 2 seconds up, 2 seconds down). The tempo ensures the muscle is actively working and not relying on momentum. The tempo also creates 'time under tension' with a continuous muscular contraction. It is the time under tension which allows for this low load training strategy. As time under tension is important, the prescription of repetitions or time is equally as effective to meet the training objective, as long as there are enough stimuli within the exercise prescription.

This type of training is ideal for inclusion when preparing for the other modalities of strength training as it gradually increases the intensity from warming up into the more intense lifting. There are often movements within this strength condition programme which are those completed within the training programme, such as squatting, pressing and pulling actions. This allows the rower to rehearse the movement and ensure there is technical excellence under lower loads which can then be transferred to higher loaded exercises. A sample exercise programme that is focused on developing load tolerance through the hip, lumbar spine and chest wall (rib cage) is shown in Fig. 6.10. In winter preparation this programme can be repeated twice, or a second circuit can be designed to increase the conditioning to 16 minutes. As rowers get closer to pre- or in season, this can drop to 4–5 minutes, continuing to load but with a reduced training volume.

Specific strength conditioning

The ergometer is a great tool for specific strength and conditioning and it just requires an imaginative coach and rower to find the right individual exercises. The same principles of overload and increasing complexity apply to these exercises; therefore the ergometer can be adapted to provide an overload. The simplest way is to increase the drag setting on the machine. Other methods are to tie the handle in place for isometric work (muscular contraction without a change in muscle length), or to use a rope and the body weight of the coach to add extra resistance through both the drive and recovery phase for both concentric (muscle contraction where the muscle shortens such as the biceps musculature during a bicep curl) and eccentric work (muscle contraction where the muscle lengthens such as the triceps musculature during a bicep curl). Reducing the gearing and drag of the ergometer to make the load lighter can also be used for speed and reaction drills.

Ergometers can also be modified and attached to weight stacks and used very effectively for seated rows at varying slide lengths.

Strength Training

Example exercises
Static suspended ergometer at the catch
Static suspended ergometer at three-quarters drive
Building from the front turn with the highest possible gearing
Building from the front turn with the lowest possible gearing
Building from the front turn on sliders or a moving head ergometer
Suspended overload drive phase

Coaching cues:
- Use form as your guide – when it is lost the rower needs to reset.

Fig. 6.11: Static suspended ergometer at the catch.

Fig. 6.12: Static suspended ergometer at three-quarters drive.

Strength Training

- If the rower's knees come together focus on the gluteal medius to bring the knees back into alignment.
- Keep the drive down low in the hips.

Putting it all together

There are no hard and fast rules around how to put a strength and conditioning training programme together. The only rule to follow is to train the adaptation and not the exercise. What is meant by that is if, for example, high force expression is the goal of the training programme, ensure the training programme is genuinely developing that physical quality. It is easy to get caught up with an exercise-led training programme, which can often lead to a single exercise being used regardless of the load, and suggesting that because that exercise is being used it is heavy strength training. As demonstrated earlier in the chapter, this is simply not the case. If a rower's legs need to have a higher force expression, prescribe exercises which follow the guidelines listed in Fig. 6.3. That way, the programme will always be focused on the outcome.

During the winter training months, decide what the goals are. Some rowers will need increases in lean muscle mass, others significant increases in strength or explosive strength. Knowing how long there is to develop these qualities will determine how the programme is organized. Remember how long it can take to make changes. For instance, hypertrophy training programmes can take an entire season to see real changes but generally 10–16 weeks to see increases of 2–3kg. When organizing training programmes, mixing heavy strength training and explosive strength training within a session (Fig. 6.7) or within a training week is a good way to ensure the rower is able to utilize the high force expression development from heavy strength training in an explosive manner. During the winter months, there may need to be greater emphasis on heavy strength training with a slightly greater emphasis on explosive strength training as rowers start closing in on the start of the season.

However, maximal force expression is a skill as much as it is a physical quality. A rower who does not regularly complete heavy strength training will quickly lose the ability to express maximal force, which is known to be a contributing factor to how fast a rower can row. Female rowers tend to lose this quality more quickly than males and also tend to take longer to regain the qualities. Rowers with less training history also tend to lose these qualities quickly and take longer to regain them. A later section in this chapter will go into more detail around the developing rower, but those rowers with a short strength training history would benefit from spending the majority of their time developing high force expression abilities (heavy strength training) throughout the entire season. In fact, for the majority of rowers, maintaining some heavy strength training in the programme throughout the season would be beneficial so that the rower does not lose the skill and physical ability to express large forces.

Another consideration to be aware of is working with lightweight rowers. While a lightweight rower may not undertake a specific hypertrophy training programme, lightweight rowers tend to respond to all strength training modalities in terms of increasing strength and lean muscle mass. While the increases in lean muscle mass may be moderate (less than 1.5kg), the added increase in total mass can become problematic when a lightweight rower is attempting to make weight for racing and regattas. The increase in lean mass may put excessive pressure on trying to reduce total mass. It is possible that while total mass has not changed, lean muscle mass has increased and body fat mass reduced. The rower's strategy of making weight may need to be altered as there

Strength Training

is less fat mass to safely and effectively reduce for competition. If the lightweight rower is unaware of these subtle changes in his morphology and tends to start the weight-making strategy very close to competition, he is likely to experience difficulty in making the desired weight.

Consistent monitoring of lightweight rowers is necessary as body composition may have changed but not total body mass. There are some ways to manage the likelihood of small to moderate increases in mass through strength training. Higher volume work such as multiple sets of 8–10 repetitions tend to be potent in increasing lean muscle mass for lightweight rowers. Recommendations would be to reduce the time a lightweight rower is using higher volume heavy strength training. As previously mentioned, no single session will suddenly increase lean muscle mass as this occurs as a result of the accumulation of work. So, having small periods of time with higher volume is acceptable, but extended periods are likely to cause unwanted hypertrophic effects.

Another point to mention is that the upper bodies of lightweight male rowers tend to respond quicker than the lower body. Small exposures to upper body volume will also help to maintain a suitable total body mass without excessive lean muscle mass. It should be noted that the high force expression capabilities are rarely if ever affected by keeping a lightweight rower away from a higher volume of heavy strength training and concentrating efforts on 3–4 sets of 1–6 repetitions.

Technique vs load

Fig. 6.13 shows the force-time curves of a non-rowing athlete back squatting with two different loads. The blue line is a 60kg back squat performed with excellent technique, while the red line is the same athlete squatting 70kg with poor technique. The 70kg lift is closer to that athlete's maximal load. The graph shows that when an athlete uses a slightly lighter load but with excellent technique, not only is the peak force significantly greater than with the

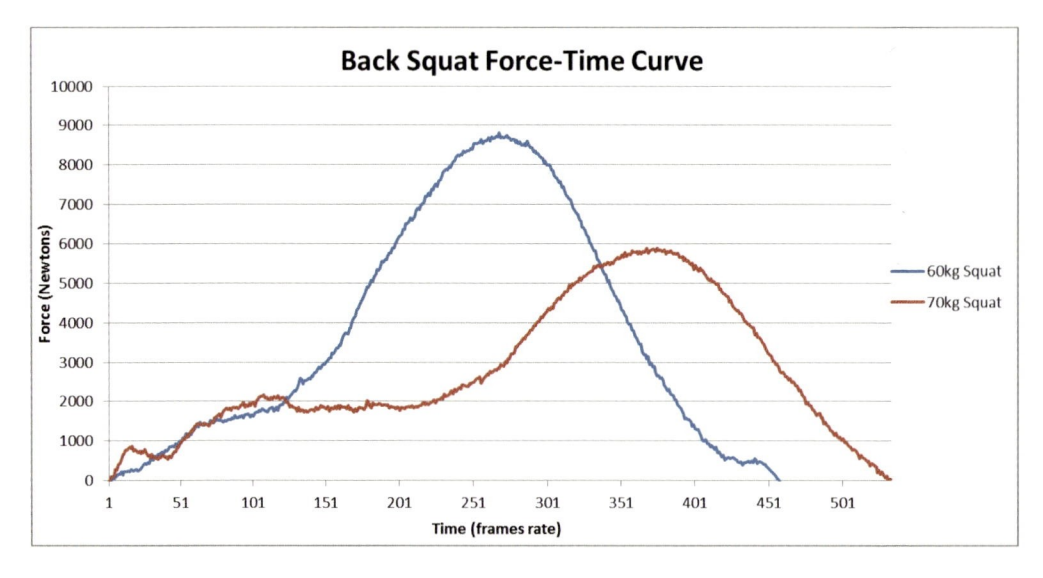

Fig. 6.13: Force-time curve of an athlete performing a back squat at two different loads.

Strength Training

heavier load, the rate (speed) at which the peak force is reached is also quicker. When an athlete has poor technique, his ability to produce large forces becomes limited. A key principle of adaptation for maximal strength training is mechanical stress, which can be measured by the amount of force the rower can produce, similar to that shown in Fig. 6.13. With mechanical stress being a primary goal, having a rower complete the exercise with technical excellence also allows for greater and more appropriate mechanical stress that will be more efficient in eliciting the key adaptations that are being trained and are required for the training objective. As described earlier, the goal of strength training is to develop the force-producing capabilities, including the rate at which force can be produced. This is an important point to consider when selecting the loads used for a rower to train with, bearing in mind that poor technique under greater loads can negatively impact the development and expression of force-producing capabilities. It is therefore not necessary to continually strength train with a rower's maximal load on the bar for the given repetitions prescribed. It is, however, necessary to have a suitable load to gain the appropriate strength adaptation, so there is a delicate balance between load and technique. As described earlier in the chapter, loads should be at or greater than 80 per cent of the rower's maximal capability to ensure appropriate adaptation is gained from heavy strength training. Too heavy a load may result in poor technique; too light is not enough to create change.

Concurrent training

There is a clear need for rowers to have a very strong aerobic endurance capability, as described in earlier chapters. However, there is also a need to develop the anaerobic strength training physical qualities due to the physical demands of rowing. All other things being equal (technique and aerobic fitness), the rower who is more forceful will have a greater economy, so will be working a lower percentage of a muscle's maximal capacity for a given rowing speed or stroke rate. The rower will also have a greater ability to maximally exert force, which becomes important for the first one to ten strokes of a race (particularly for lightweights) and sprints to the finish line. Unfortunately, training both endurance and strength simultaneously within the same training day or week has conflicting adaptation processes.

There is plenty of evidence demonstrating that endurance performance or adaptation is not necessarily affected by the inclusion of strength training. On the contrary, as noted previously, endurance performance has been shown to be improved with the addition of strength training. However, the same cannot be said for strength adaptation and performance. High volume endurance training can blunt the adaptation from strength training, whether this is the ability for a group of muscles to produce large forces or trying to increase the mass of the musculature. It is therefore essential that the rower optimizes the adaptation of both endurance and strength training through appropriate planning of the programme and nutrition.

When looking at organizing training throughout the day, it is possible to make significant gains in both strength and muscle mass by strength training in the morning, followed by endurance training with the appropriate recovery between sessions; this can be later that morning or in the afternoon. The premise for this is that the rower's body has recovered more from the last training session, which is normally over 12 hours earlier. The rower would be able to nutritionally recover, and there is also a period of enforced recovery in sleeping.

It is possible to make the same significant changes in strength and muscle mass by employing strength training as the last session of the day. While the rower may have been subjected to one or two other sessions during the day and will carry fatigue into the strength training session, he will have the longest period post-training to adapt before embarking on the next training session the following day. There is evidence to suggest that the last training stimulus of the day is the one to which the body will adapt over previous training stimuli. Therefore, if strength or muscle mass are significant priorities, completing strength training as the last session of the day would be advisable. This is where the greatest success has been achieved with athletes from multiple sports when in a concurrent training programme. It is important to note that there are clear recovery periods between sessions earlier in the day so there is also time for the rowers to adapt from endurance sessions completed earlier in the day. In addition, rowers will always have a significantly greater amount of endurance training over strength training throughout the week and potentially days where no strength training is completed. This provides plenty of opportunities for the rower to still adapt to the endurance training while prioritizing adaptation from strength training.

A final important note is that the least successful strength and muscle mass adaptations have occurred when the strength training session has been sandwiched between two endurance training sessions within a day. Previous experience has continually shown the limited impact of this training organization. Placing a strength training session at either end of the day would be advisable to optimize the adaptations planned from this training, regardless of whether strength or muscle mass is the goal. As previously stated, if there is limited time dedicated to strength training and it is always competing against a higher volume of endurance training, the strength gains can be compromised. Therefore, it is critical to optimize training adaptation so that the impact of the training can be experienced by the rower during training and, more importantly, competition. In Chapter 11, some general considerations will be made around the nutritional strategies that can further optimize the adaptations from strength training.

Strength training for the developing rower

The previous sections in this chapter have been tailored for rowers who have an extensive history of strength training. The sections that provide specific examples of training programmes are therefore aimed at those with at least two to three years of training and who are fully matured. The rationale for this is that the programmes listed will create a large amount of mechanical stress across joints and through the musculature. For those who have not experienced maximal loading, this can be very stressful. For a rower who has yet to fully mature, maximal loading is not recommended because of the adverse effects this can have on developing joints, including bone development and soft tissue (muscles, tendons and ligaments).

Furthermore, focusing on load over form as depicted in the hierarchy of loading in Fig. 6.2 does not allow rowers to develop fundamental movement quality and depth of physical literacy. The developing rower who spends more time concentrating on the load lifted instead of the quality and variability of exercise selection will ultimately limit his own trainability. 'Trainability' is the ability for a rower to use multiple training modalities to gain a similar training adaptation.

For instance, a rower who may have an injured wrist may not be able to use power cleans as a training stimulus to develop explosive strength. If he has been exposed to a variety of quality controlled jumping exercises he could supplement the training programme with loaded jump squats to elicit the similar triple extension explosive strength pattern to the power clean. A rower who has failed to be exposed to multiple types of training including fundamentals like jumping would not be able to load the jump effectively (heavily enough) to gain the same training adaptation. To illustrate further, a rower who can clean 100kg would be expected to loaded jump squat 65–75kg. A rower who has had this type of training included earlier in his training career would probably reach that target with ease within a couple of sessions. However, novice jumpers would spend the entirety of the time (or at least a large proportion of it) that they are unable to clean learning how to jump effectively, which has a significant impact on the explosive strength adaptation. As identified in Fig. 6.4, rowers need to train the adaptation and not the exercise; therefore, creating the correct load, speed and volume is critical. Simply replacing one exercise with another will not necessarily create the same adaptation unless the guidelines are followed and the rower is capable of completing a similar exercise in the first place, which comes back to his trainability as a developing rower.

All developing rowers should spend time completing body weight exercises in the early phases of training. This should include press-ups, supine pulls, assisted chin-ups (or even unassisted in some cases), lunge/step patterns, squat patterns, crawling patterns, jump take-offs and landings, and hop take-offs and landings. This will provide the foundation of all movements that a rower is likely to experience in his athletic career. While it is abundantly clear that there is a crossover between a press-up and bench press, it is often neglected. For instance, rowers and athletes from other sports like completing bench press over press-ups. There is significant evidence from research literature showing that when completing a press-up, the subject is lifting 60–70 per cent of their body mass. For example, if a 75kg female rower's press-up is two thirds of her body mass (66 per cent), the load going through the shoulder girdle is around 50kg. Yet when the rower is bench pressing, the typical load used is 40kg or less for similar repetitions. For the bench press to be truly effective, the load needs to be significantly greater than two thirds (60–70 per cent) of the rower's body mass to consider using it as a training modality. This rower would benefit spending more time developing press-up capability through inclines or starting from knees. Allowing development rowers to use body weight exercises allows them to explore movement variations and challenges while also setting them up to transfer to barbell lifting under load.

While circuit training is not strictly strength training (see Fig. 6.4), it is an excellent way to start incorporating the body weight movement patterns as described above. This is particularly important in any type of strength training for novices. However, while traditionally the focus of circuit training has been around developing aerobic or local muscular endurance capacity, the focus for the novice rower should be on the quality of movement. The rower should be able to have progressions and regressions within a circuit to allow him to progress accordingly. The message to the rower about the quality should be reinforced and 'grinding out' the session should be avoided. Completing well executed movements under a little fatigue can be just as physically challenging as completing multiple repetitions without regard to technique to create local muscular endurance or aerobic adaptation.

Developing rowers should spend time mastering technical competency of major barbell lifts (squats, deadlifts, bench press, bench pull and Olympic lifts such as the snatch, clean and jerk). It cannot be stressed enough that technical mastery of these lifts will set up a rower for the rest of his athletic career and help facilitate training adaptation significantly more effectively than without it. When a coach is observing on-water rowing, the rower is appraised against a technical model of excellence. The coach will know what an 'excellent' position looks like at the catch and mid-drive phases. The coach will also know what 'excellent' movement from catch to mid-drive looks like. This level of understanding is fundamental to all coaching regardless of the sport, task or skill being coached. Weightlifting is no different. Understanding what an 'excellent' technical model is for the power clean is just as critical for long-term athlete development in the gym as an 'excellent' technical model for the rowing stroke in a boat. Developing a knowledge of weightlifting technique may require additional support from a weightlifting or strength and conditioning coach, but this will pay off in the future by preventing the limiting of training adaptation through poor technique.

Experience has shown that poor training history as a developing athlete has blunted physical capability as a senior athlete, both in rowing and in other sports. An example from another sport saw a 14-week pre-season training block spent teaching those who had no history of lifting to safely lift; only after 12–14 weeks did the athletes start to see meaningful changes in maximal strength, explosive strength and running acceleration. It took another two years before there were significant changes in their physical qualities. Their competitors would have spent the same time refining the physical capabilities to optimize performance on the field. Those with some experience of lifting but with poor technique spent the entirety of that 14-week pre-season unpicking the habits that had been ingrained. Some of the athletes were never able to fully return to a technically excellent model, which limited their training adaptation and response to training. It could be argued that poor technical competency is potentially worse than having a limited training history, as reversing the ingrained habits is more difficult to overcome than teaching afresh. It should be clear just how important working on technical competency both in the gym and on the water is as a developing rower, creating an almost physically limitless rower and a crew maker.

Barbell lifting can be introduced simultaneously with body weight exercises: there is no graduation from one to the next. As stated earlier in this section, maximal loading to failure should be avoided to reduce risk of injury to immature bones, joints and soft tissue, and due to those in the early phases of lifting having a lack of awareness around intent and control of larger loads. It is not advisable to do maximum testing. Simply tracking the load on the bar week by week will give the best indication of how the rower is progressing. Using power strokes or short ergometer sprints (see Chapter 7) will also help to show the impact of the training on the ergometer, which is a closer resemblance to rowing itself. A system of being able to review an athlete's technical competency while lifting under load has been termed 'technical strength deficit'. If a rower completes a perfect back squat using the technical guidelines in Chapter 9, they are given 100 per cent. The rower increases the load and again the coach appraises the technical competency. If the rower again hits 100 per cent, the load can increase. However, if with the increased load the rower drops to, say, 70 per cent competency as the hips rise before the bar moves at the start of the ascent and the back is slightly rounded, the rower has hit his technical strength deficit. This is the point at which the rower is unable to lift any more without compromising the technical competency for performance, but also for safety. The rower then drops down to a weight where he

Strength Training

can maintain competency. He can regularly try to exceed the technical strength deficit and if successful continue to work at the new load. This provides a useful tool to help develop a rower who can withstand repeated loading while maintaining technical competency, while also providing a framework for coaches and rowers alike to determine when it is safe to increase the load.

As rowers become more experienced with lifting, including maintaining technical competency under increasing loads, the rower can start to develop into the types of programmes outlined above. For a rower to be able to competently complete these types of programmes, two to three years of strength training history should have been achieved, with care taken for those who have not yet met full maturation. While it is still possible to complete the programmes in late stages of maturation, it is advised that the very top end of maximal loading and testing be reserved for those who are fully mature with two to three years of strength training history.

Intent

Intent is an area that is often forgotten about when designing a training programme, both on the water and in the gym. Intent describes the directed mental effort required to achieve the training objective or outcome. For instance, lifting 5 sets of 5 repetitions for the back squat at a load which is maximal for that repetition range is hugely stressful and requires the rower to truly focus on the lift. It is easy for a rower to put 5–10kg less on the bar and complete the volume, but the rower may have limited the outcome of the session. If the rower could lift more while maintaining excellent technical competency, the directed mental effort or the rower's intent to do so is absolutely critical. This means the rower must focus on the lifting and nothing else. Part of this is creating the environment for the rower to do this. Organizing rowers in groups where they can work together to get the best out of themselves and each other is important. Creating a lifting environment where rowers feel safe and compelled to demonstrate intent is also important. This requires rowers to understand how to fail and spot safely (see Chapter 7). Music and lighting can also create an environment which allows rowers to excel.

Organization of the training programme can help as well. For instance, if you want the rower to maintain a very high degree of intent for heavy strength training, it is not advisable to superset or supplement the exercise with low level exercises where the rower is removed from the high intensity. Keeping the rower at a high degree of intent is easier than going from high to low and back again – it is exhausting to have to keep raising the mental effort multiple times within a session. The warm-up should naturally lead into more intense work, requiring the rower to continue to increase their intent. This is a skill and with practice rowers can become excellent at it and are capable of leading it themselves. While rowers are developing their skills with strength training, providing opportunities for the rowers to explore this is important. It can simply be done by allowing the rowers to provide appropriate music, understand how they like to receive feedback and create a working environment that gets the best out of them.

Functional strength training

Much has been said about functional strength training over the past decade or even longer. Some strength and conditioning coaches and those specializing in physical preparation have advocated that the weight room should replicate the movement the athlete or rower is performing in the event itself. This has led to exercises that start to look like rowing

Strength Training

in the weight room. At first glance, this may seem like a good idea to implement as the 'movement' itself is similar to the sport of rowing. However, on closer inspection, there are significant differences between exercise selection and rowing itself. While there are numerous reasons given as to why this may not be the most optimal way to train, the two areas to focus on are motor learning and overload.

Motor learning, in simple terms, is the body's ability to learn and refine a skill or series of skills. When the body is exposed to a new task, the brain will recall previous strategies which are similar to that currently being completed. This is an effective way to chunk movement patterns together to increase the speed of learning and execution of the task. When a skill such as the rowing stroke is repeatedly completed, the rower will become an expert in the technical model. From the outside, the coach will see a rockover at the start of the recovery and all the associated positions during the remainder of the recovery phase and completion of the drive phase. However, at a local level (i.e. at a cellular level), what is not seen is the coordination within and between muscles, such as a co-contraction of the quad and hamstring to extend the knee during the drive phase. The coordination component within and between muscles is an important consideration as this becomes a finely tuned skill of specific timing of contractions in terms of the speed and magnitude between the muscles. It is like a world class orchestra where all the musicians are in harmony contributing to a Beethoven symphony. However, when the coordination of muscular contractions becomes out of sync or is misfiring, the fluidity of the rowing stroke becomes compromised, which reduces the technical excellence of the rower. This would be akin to the woodwind section joining the symphony out of time or playing the wrong part.

There is a real danger of compromising the fluidity of the rowing stroke by trying to replicate the entire stroke or even a part of it in the weight room by using exercises which mimic the exact action of the stroke. There are resistance machines that have tried to replicate the rowing stroke action. The increase in load is likely to be greater than the actual rowing stroke but not heavy enough to overload the rower to make significant changes in strength quality, and has the potential to change the coordinative interaction within and between muscles as the timing and magnitude within and between muscles may be altered. This could then cross over into the rowing stroke during water or ergometer training.

Secondly, the primary focus around strength training is to change the physical output, whether that be a higher force (heavy strength training) or higher power (explosive strength training). To do this effectively, the rower must have progressive overload within the training programme. Progressive overload is where the exercise stresses the rower enough to create a force or power change (in simple terms, how hard a muscle can contract or how quickly it can contract). The load has to be greater than that which the rower has experienced before and significantly greater than that experienced while rowing for it to be effective in changing the capability of the muscle being trained. Using exercises that mimic the rowing stroke rarely significantly overload any of the muscles required during the rowing stroke. It is the overload being significantly greater than the event demands itself which elicits the training adaptations necessary to improve the rower's performance for force and power application. Slightly overloading a group or series of muscles beyond the level experienced in the rowing stroke may have some strength conditioning or local muscular endurance effect (if a high enough volume of it is completed) but will not alter force and power capability.

Strength Training

If the goal for a rower is to develop a greater leg extension force application, then heavy strength training should be prescribed. To go one step further, if the limiting factor to heavy squatting or deadlifting is the lumbar back load, then the legs will only ever be exposed to what the lumbar spine can tolerate. This limits the force development of the legs. However, allowing the rower to use a leg press to increase leg extension force removes the lumbar back tolerance issue and therefore the legs are exposed to greater loading. Using the functional training model would dismiss the use of machine weights, which can be very useful for training. The use of machine weights is particularly helpful when trying to target hypertrophy gains of specific parts of the body such as the quadriceps musculature, where the leg extension may be the most optimal exercise to create a change in lean muscle mass.

A good analogy would be a male rower who squats 130kg for 5 repetitions, using 60 per cent of the maximal force capacity around the gluteal musculature and 50 per cent through the quadriceps musculature, but the lumbar back is working at 95 per cent of its maximal capacity. For the rower to move to 140kg to increase the gluteal and quadriceps musculature capacity, the lumbar back would have to work at 105 per cent of its maximal capacity. Firstly, this puts the rower at risk of injuring the lumbar spine, and secondly, the legs are limited by the lumbar back tolerance so cannot load the legs effectively enough to elicit high force adaptations.

There has been a tradition of allowing rowers to squat with narrow feet as if in a boat. Again, while the original premise for this was probably about increasing transfer of training, the reality is the rower is put into a significantly weaker position to squat. It increases the load through the lumbar back by increasing the trunk lean during the decent and ascent, reduces the depth of squat for many due to the architecture of the hip joint, increases the need for a knee- and not hip-dominant action and ultimately reduces the load a rower can use, which is necessary to elicit the high force adaptation required to improve rowing performance. Some rowers are capable of squatting with a narrow stance with excellent technical competency and without compromise to the lumbar back. However, these rowers are the exception and not the norm and should not be used as a reason for all rowers to squat like this. These rowers are genetically gifted in that hip architecture and joint mobility are not limiting factors. For the rest, using the guidelines in Chapter 9 to set up for an optimal squat position is the basis to start from. Allow rowers to explore the position that allows them to load safely and effectively.

CHAPTER 7

MONITORING AND ASSESSING LAND TRAINING

A rower's training adaptations and his training programme need to be constantly reviewed to assess whether the programme aims are being achieved. There is a distinction between monitoring of training and testing performance.

Monitoring of training may consist of tracking aerobic fitness gains by conducting incremental step tests or submaximal ergometer tests that are measured either by oxygen consumption or lactate accumulation. You need a physical load and a physiological marker that can be measured. Whichever method you choose, it has to be accurate, repeatable and reliable.

Performance testing is as specific a test as you can get both on the water and on the ergometer. For the rower looking for a 2,000m performance, a 2,000m ergometer test or a 6-minute test is ideal. Different performance tests can happen during the various training phases. 5,000m and 6,000m tests are popular tools for the winter period. These tests are at maximal effort and usually done with free rate.

Testing on the water covers similar distances to ergometer performance tests and helps the coach and rower build a measure of performance progress. 250m, 500m, 1,000m, 1,500m, 2,000m and 5,000m tests are all used to assess boat speed progression and development.

The coach and rower can develop a simple, effective monitoring and testing regime that can track the rower's training and performance development by selecting a series of distances on the ergometer that the rower is able to move through on the physiological ladder, from short anaerobic to long endurance pieces.

This provides valuable information to identify if the rower is more aerobically or anaerobically predominant. This can help the coach and rower target the training that is most needed for the rower's improvement (Fig. 7.1).

The most effective way to monitor a rower's workload is by looking at the watts or split he pulls on the ergometer. Most ergometer brands are reliable in this area.

There are two other components that need to be added to complete a picture of a rower's training progression. Against the workload there needs to be a physiological cost so that the rower's effort can be assessed. There are many ways this can be done, from the simple measurement of heart rate, to lactates and going into the laboratory for oxygen consumption testing. Physiological monitoring tools such as heart rate monitors and lactate analyzers are becoming more and more affordable and useable, and also come with clever software that can be used to track the rower's progression.

The final marker is the athlete's perception of the workload. A perceived exertion scale from 1 to 10 can work very well, or you can use the normal feeling of a split he pulls on the ergometer. There are some different perceived exertion charts available to use. The Borg scale combines heart rate with perceived exertion, which is a useful combination.

In developing your monitoring programme there is a monitoring triad you can keep in mind, as set out in Fig. 7.2. If the rower is taking the training in his stride, all three elements

Monitoring and Assessing Land Training

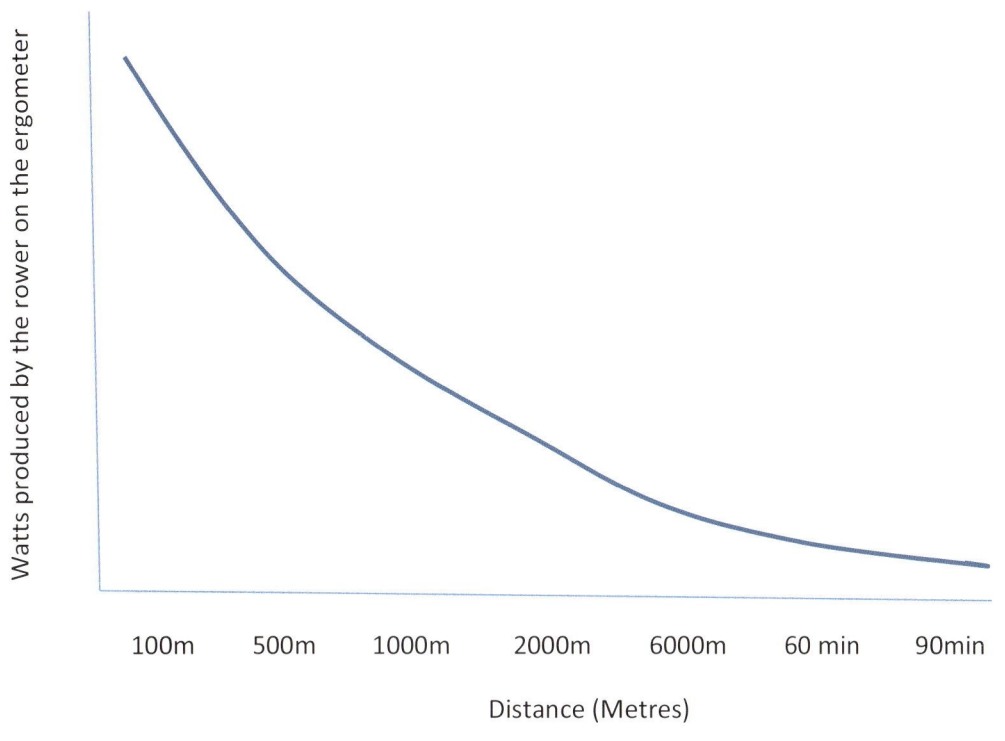

Fig. 7.1: Power profile.

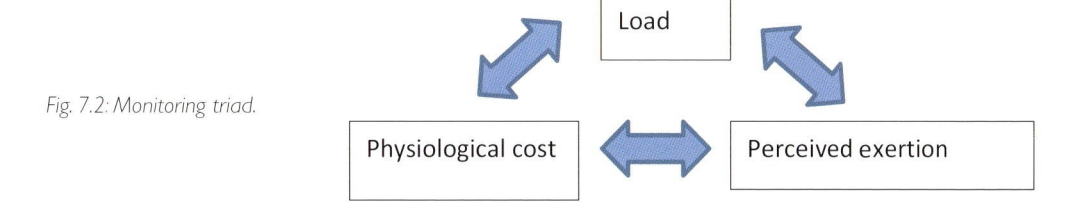

Fig. 7.2: Monitoring triad.

Monitoring and Assessing Land Training

should be in balance. His physiological cost is in keeping with the load and the split on the ergometer. His feel for the split should be something he would describe as normal. Often, if the rower's feeling is not normal, illness can be around the corner.

If the rower is out of balance and has either overstretched his training or succumbed to illness, the best way to bring him back is to focus on normalizing his steady state training and getting the perception/load/cost monitoring triad back in balance. Once this is achieved, higher intensity and more volume of training can be undertaken.

Strength training testing

Heavy strength training

It is possible to measure a rower's progress in the weight room by monitoring the training weight he uses week by week. Increasing weight on the bar demonstrates that a rower has become stronger. However, if necessary, the rower can complete a repetition maximum (RM) test, where he will perform a low number of repetitions (1–5) to ascertain his current RM. Fig. 7.3 shows the coefficient factors that can be used to identify a predicted 1RM based on the number of repetitions lifted. This can be used within a standard training set as a gauge of where the rower is or as a standalone testing session. Identify the number of repetitions lifted between 1 and 10 and then multiply the load lifted with the coefficient factor corresponding to the number of repetitions lifted. For instance, a male rower who lifted 80kg for 3 repetitions in the bench press would multiply 80kg by 1.09, the coefficient for 3 repetitions. This would predict the rower's 1RM to be 87.2kg. Since the majority of weights within the weight room are in 1.25kg increments, this can be rounded up to 87.5kg. The limitation of this formula and all

Repetitions	Coefficient
1	1.00
2	1.04
3	1.09
4	1.13
5	1.18
6	1.22
7	1.25
8	1.29
9	1.33
10	1.36

Fig. 7.3: 1RM prediction coefficients.

other predictive equations is the gradual inaccuracy if trying to predict a 1RM for exercises where the rower may have lifted 6 or more repetitions. Fig. 7.3 is fairly representative of a predictive 1RM from 5 repetitions or less but there will be a degree of inaccuracy as repetitions increase in predicting 1RM. This must be taken into consideration when using this coefficient system.

If a rower completes this test to his maximal ability, it is very stressful and should not be performed regularly. Although completing a 3RM test as opposed to a 1RM test involves less load, the stress is much greater due to the larger number of repetitions. Only well trained, skilled lifters should perform this type of testing. As with all testing, the rower should be well warmed up, practising the exercise movement with increasing loads. While it is a rower's choice as to exactly how many near-maximal effort repetitions are completed as part of the warm-up, it is suggested to include 2–3 single repetitions of increasing weight building from around 80 to 95 per cent of the load the rower is intending to lift during the testing. Allowing a rower to have 3–4 maximal efforts is ideal, as with any more the risk of injury starts to increase as the rower becomes more fatigued. Rowers will also need 5–6 minutes to recover between efforts, so managing time is also important. If completing multiple testing lifts

Monitoring and Assessing Land Training

Repetitions	Percentage of 1RM	Coefficient
1	100%	1
2	95%	0.95
3	93%	0.93
4	90%	0.9
5	87%	0.87
6	85%	0.85
7	82%	0.82
8	80%	0.8
9	77%	0.77
10	75%	0.75

Fig. 7.4: 1RM testing multiplication factors to prescribe training loads.

within a session, this also increases the time commitment required.

Once a rower has established a 1RM through testing or through the predictive system outlined in Fig. 7.3, it is possible to then prescribe training loads based on this information. Fig. 7.4 is an extension of Fig. 6.4 in the previous chapter, with the addition of a coefficient column which can be used to ascertain a training load based on a real or predicted 1RM. For instance, using the previous example above of a male rower with a predicted 1RM of 87.5kg in the bench press, to ascertain a training load for 6 repetitions, multiply 87.5kg by 0.85 (coefficient for 6 repetitions). This would provide a training load of 74.4kg. Again, rounding to the nearest 1.25kg would give the rower a training load for 6 repetitions of 75kg. As with the previous coefficient system to establish 1RM, using this system to identify a training load is equally susceptible to inaccuracy. The greater the number of repetitions, the greater the inaccuracy. This again should be taken into account when prescribing training loads, especially those of 6 repetitions or more.

Explosive strength training

Power testing can be relatively simple and inexpensive for a rowing programme. Using an ergometer, it is possible to ascertain increases in power using short sprints such as a 7–10 power stroke protocol or a 100m ergo sprint. It is important to measure watts rather than split as this provides a greater degree of accuracy. The rower can also perform countermovement jumps on contact mats, or standing horizontal broad jumps for distance, both of which have been validated as measures of power (explosive strength). The higher or further a rower jumps, the more powerful he is. There is a degree of familiarization to jump testing, so it is advisable to allow the rower to incorporate several jumps within the warm-up. Explosive strength training measurement is highly sensitive to fatigue from high intensity bouts within a warm-up or a series of previously completed jump trials. If a rower is given an opportunity to practise jumping prior to testing, ensure he has 3–5 minutes recovery before completing the testing. You should take the best distance of the 3–5 trials completed.

Hypertrophy

Testing for increases in body mass is the simplest of all testing completed, as all that is required is an accurate set of weighing scales, and most boat clubs will have a set for lightweight rowers to use to regularly monitor body mass. This is the easiest way to measure increases in body mass. However, what this does not identify are changes in body fat and lean muscle mass. Having a skilled practitioner (e.g. one who is International Society for the Advancement of Kinanthropometry (ISAK) Level 1 accredited) to measure the changes will allow a greater depth of knowledge of where any mass increase has come from, such as by undertaking skinfold testing, which measures body fat, and girth measurements (combined lean muscle mass and fat mass). From these two assessments the amount of muscle mass at specific sites around the body can be determined. Please refer to the ISAK website for more details: http://www.isakonline.com/

Monitoring and Assessing Land Training

There are multiple other methods that can be used to determine changes in mass and body composition; however, they are often very expensive (found in medical institutions, such as dual-energy x-ray absorptiometry [DEXA]) and require skilled technicians to complete the assessment. The cheaper bioimpedance systems, where a rower grips a device or stands barefoot on something similar to scales to measure safe low frequency electrical current through the body, are open to error. By measuring the electrical impedance, the result implies the level of body fat within the body. However, the hydration and electrolyte status of a rower may interfere with the results. Therefore, if this system is being used, trying to test the rower at a time where he is likely to be in the same hydrated state each time is important. For instance, you would get variable results if on one Monday the test was completed pre-training and the following Monday it was completed post-training.

Pre-test protocols

To make the results of monitoring and testing as reliable as possible, it is best practice to standardize as much as possible the training and physiological state of the rower before his testing and monitoring commences. Rules of thumb are to test at a similar time in the day, with the rower following a similar diet on the day. Pre-test training should be steady state; don't do weights pre-test and do the same pre-test training before each test. This will help to provide consistency for the monitoring and testing so that the results will be more accurate and reliable. It is also advantageous to make monitoring and testing part of your training. Often programmes can consist of only preparation for testing and the testing itself, not leaving enough time for solid training.

Post-testing

Assessing the results of testing is a skill, but the key is what to do with them. When the results come back, what is going to change in the rower's training? Often coaches have the same response, whether testing results come back that have been encouraging or have shown that the rower has regressed, with the answer being 'more training'. That may be what is required, but if a rower comes back in good shape, with a positive improvement in his performance, you may consider whether all the benefit possible has been gained from the training stimulus you have been using, and whether you need to provide another form of training stimulus to keep the improvement going.

If a test comes back and the rower has regressed, firstly you need to ascertain his health status. Is he ill? Has he been injured? Is he doing the full programme? Is he doing the programme correctly? Is his slow work too fast and his fast work too slow? How has his test compared to the rest of the group or crew? Having established these parameters, you need to consider which strategy you will take to turn things around.

How often should you test and monitor training?

Some form of monitoring – assessing the rower's readiness and ability to train and do the programme – should be ongoing and weekly. A performance test should mark the end of a training block, to assess the effectiveness and adaptation achieved.

CHAPTER 8

MOBILITY AND FLEXIBILITY

Chapter 2 started to outline the importance of the delicate balance between trunk strength and control alongside the importance of range of movement necessary for an effective rowing technical model. Chapter 10 identifies the requirements for having a strong and functional trunk for rowing. This chapter will focus on mobility and flexibility.

It is important to define the difference between mobility and flexibility, as these terms are sometimes incorrectly used to describe the same thing. Mobility is concerned with the range of movement around a joint. This can be affected by a number of things, such as anatomical structure where the joint cannot rotate any further (such as the elbow not extending much further than straight arm), pain inhibition from an injury, or central nervous system control stopping the joint rotating fully to protect itself from injury and muscle length. This is not an exhaustive list, but it highlights the fact that mobility is multi-faceted, with a number of anatomical and physiological constraints to overcome. Flexibility, however, refers purely to muscle length. Muscle flexibility is a component of mobility and as such is an exercise modality to improve mobility around a joint.

Throughout this chapter, we highlight a variety of methods to improve mobility that have been found to be very effective for rowers. While we will not exhaust every possible exercise within a specific type of mobility, the principles behind each type can be transferred to almost any joint or body segment. For instance, the principles of foam rolling the hip flexor musculature (see Fig. 8.4) are the same for foam rolling the gastrocnemius (lower leg) musculature. It is at the coach's and rower's discretion to determine how best to use the exercise modalities to attain the required improvements.

The rationale for focusing on the areas of the body that impact the quality of range of movement is based on the technical model for rowing. For example, a rower needs good range of movement through the hips (long hamstring musculature and freely movable hips) and at the ankle complex to allow him to attain a good rockover position at the catch. A good rockover position also requires the rower to have good length through the upper back (latissimus dorsi and surrounding musculature) and a freely movable thoracic spine. When any of these areas are compromised, the coach may see the rower reduce the length of the rowing stroke, with excessive rounding of the upper back to create the required length, or a poor rockover position. While some of this may be a result of having inadequate trunk condition to be able to hold a strong position, it can also be due to reduced range of movement around the joints and shortening of the muscles surrounding the ankle, hips, back and shoulders.

Large volumes of training put a lot of repetitive stress through the body areas listed above, which can create chronic changes in muscle lengths and in the extent to which joints are freely movable. Maintaining the required range of movement and muscle length is important

Mobility and Flexibility

so that compensatory movement patterns are not used and so that the impact (reduced range of movement and muscle length) of chronic loading through these body parts can be reversed. Both of these have implications on injury risk and technical movement competency, which ultimately change the optimal performance of the rower.

It is important that, when prescribing mobility-based exercises, you consult physiotherapists, strength and conditioning coaches or other qualified practitioners to ensure that exercise programmes are tailored to the individual rower. Not all rowers will require time spent on developing the range of movement in all areas. However, the exercises and the body areas identified below are a good starting point for most rowers as they work on all the key areas. To make substantial changes in any range of movement or muscle length, the rower must spend significant time devoted to that area. In general, each of the exercises below should be completed for a minimum of 2 minutes and upwards to 10 minutes. This may seem excessive; however, this is the most effective way to make lasting changes. It is recommended that exercises be completed daily. Prior to rowing or ergometer work, cross-training or weight training, significant time should be spent on these body areas. If completing multiple training sessions in a day, spending a large amount of time on this prior to the first session and then smaller doses on potentially problematic areas prior to the second or third sessions is recommended.

As stated earlier, it is at the coach's and rower's discretion as to how best to tailor the exercises for the rower. Completing a stand-alone mobility training session can also be used to great effect to change ranges of movements and muscle lengths. This can include the exercise modalities identified below or could use other effective modalities like yoga. While the primary goal of this type of training is to improve range of movement and muscle length, if a session is organized well it can also be a great way for a rower to relax and prepare for the next training session. It should be noted that some of the exercises below can create discomfort for the rower, particularly the foam rolling exercises. This is normal; it may take a rower a little time to get used to completing this type of exercise.

Ankle mobility

Knee to wall

Fig. 8.1: Knee to wall.

Mobility and Flexibility

The purpose of this exercise is to increase the range of movement around the ankle joint by dynamically taking the ankle through to near-terminal ankle dorsi flexion (toes moving as close to the shin as possible).

Set-up:
- Complete this exercise without shoes on.
- Place one foot about 6–10cm away from a wall, with the opposite foot about a foot length behind.
- Support body weight by leaning against the wall.

Execution:
- Push the knee of the front foot towards the wall while always maintaining the heel on the floor.
- The rower can dynamically move the knee back and forth towards the wall.

- Alternatively, the rower can maintain the position of the knee towards the wall and then sweep the knee from left to right, again keeping the heel to the floor.
- Spend the majority of the time in the areas which are most tight or lack range of movement.
- If the rower can touch the wall with his knee, move the foot further away.
- This exercise can also be used as an assessment to determine improvements in range of movement by determining the maximum distance between the front of the foot and the wall while the knee is in contact with the wall.

Hip mobility

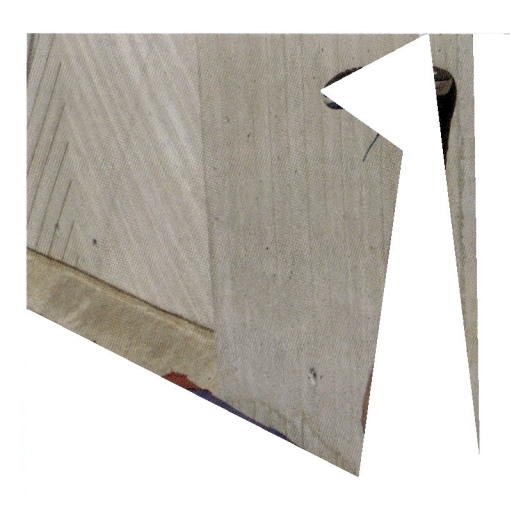

Static hamstring stretch

Fig. 8.2: Static hamstring stretch.

Mobility and Flexibility

Set-up:
- Using the corner of two walls, lie on a mat facing upwards with hips as close to the wall as possible.

Execution:
- Extend one leg up against the wall, ensuring the knee is fully extended.
- Simultaneously allow the opposite leg to drop to the floor and remain in a totally horizontal position.
- The back should remain in a flat position on the mat.
- Push the heel of the raised foot against the wall while simultaneously extending the knee for 10–15 seconds, then relax for 10 seconds. Attempt to extend knee and move leg closer to the vertical using the contract-relax timings for the desired amount of time.
- This exercise can also be used as an assessment to determine improvements in hamstring length. The perfect position for the leg against the wall is with a fully extended knee in a totally vertical position, while maintaining the opposite leg with an extended knee in a totally horizontal position. This should create a 90-degree angle between both legs. Measure the angle by simply taking a photo from side on to monitor any progression.

Gluteal musculature foam rolling

Set-up:
- Sit on the foam roller with the majority of the body weight on the gluteal musculature.
- Place the foot of the side which has most of the body weight going through the gluteal musculature onto the opposite knee.
- Place hands behind the body to support body weight.

Fig. 8.3: Gluteal musculature foam rolling.

Mobility and Flexibility

Fig. 8.4: Hip flexor foam rolling.

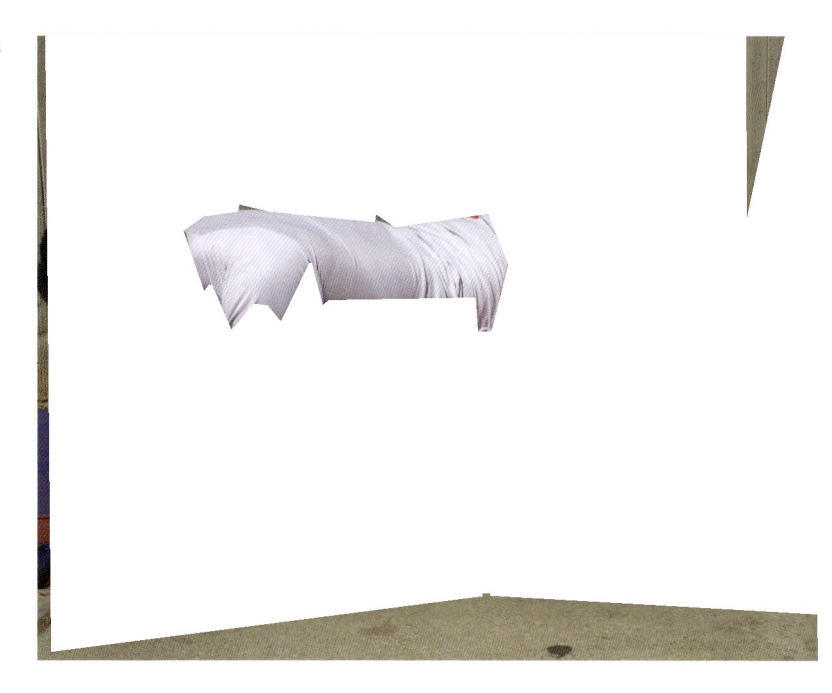

Execution:
- Slowly roll the gluteal musculature across the foam roller, making sure to work across the entire gluteal area, including the outside borders of the gluteals, down towards the buttock crease and up to the belt line.
- Either roll across the tight or sore area or maintain a static pressure on this area – this is at the rower's discretion.
- Spend the majority of the time in the areas which are most tight or sore.
- With the foot resting on the opposite knee, bring this knee closer to the chest, which increases the length of the gluteal musculature.

Hip flexor and quadriceps musculature foam rolling

Set-up:
- Lie face down with the foam roller situated on the side of the hip just below the belt line for the hip flexor, or anywhere between hip and knee for the quadriceps.
- Support body weight through forearms in a similar position to a front plank.

Execution:
- Slowly roll the top of the hip across the foam roller, making sure to include rolling on the outside of the hip for the hip flexor and down towards the knee for the quadriceps. Rolling the foam roller on the inside of the thigh just above the knee is also recommended as this area tends to become tight with rowing and with lower body strength training.
- Either roll across the tight or sore area or maintain a static pressure on this area – this is at the rower's discretion.
- Spend the majority of the time in the areas that are most tight or sore.

Mobility and Flexibility

Fig. 8.5: Thoracic extension.

Thoracic spine mobility

Dynamic extension and rotation

Set-up:

- Lie face up across a foam roller with hips on the floor and knees bent, allowing the feet to be flat on the floor.
- Let the head rest on the mat.

Execution:

- For thoracic extension, flex the arms overhead with elbows fully extended.
- Dynamically move in and out of this position, attempting to increase the range of movement with each repetition.
- For thoracic rotation, wrap the arms around yourself and slowly rotate through the thoracic spine from left to right.

- For both exercises, roll the back over the foam roller to repeat the movements, spending the majority of the time in the area which has the least range of movement or is the tightest.

Latissimus dorsi (lats)/upper back musculature dynamic stretch

Set-up:
- Anchor a 40"-long rubber band to a wall bar or something similar at a height greater than that of the rower. If a band is not available, using a boat tie can elicit similar results.
- Place the hand inside the band, taking a grip of the band.
- Step away from the anchor point until the band is under tension – this should result in the arm being fully extended at the elbow with hand above shoulder.

Mobility and Flexibility

Fig. 8.6: Latissimus dorsi dynamic stretch.

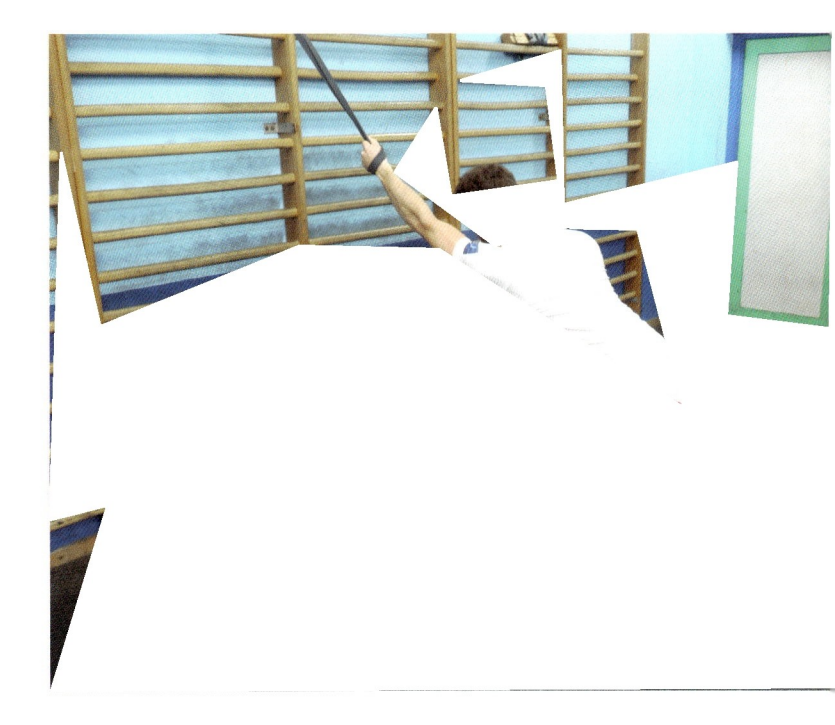

Execution:
- Flex the shoulder so the arm is above the head while simultaneously flexing at the hips, adjusting the foot position to elicit a 'stretch' across the lats.
- Continually move in and out of the position or rotate the trunk by attempting to look under the arm which is holding the band, trying to increase the range of movement with each perturbation.
- Spend the majority of the time in the areas which are most tight or sore.

As alluded to earlier in this chapter, there are a number of different modalities used to elicit improvements around ankle, hip and back mobility. These include static (contract-relax) and dynamic stretching and foam rolling (self-managed soft tissue release). There is nothing stopping the coach or rower from using variations of these techniques and the equipment with other parts of the body. For those who do not have access to a foam roller, an inexpensive alternative is taping two tennis balls together with tape making a peanut shape (see Fig. 8.7), which can be used as an

Fig. 8.7: Homemade 'peanut' using two tennis balls and tape.

87

Mobility and Flexibility

alternative for all the foam roller exercises listed and more.

Here is a link to a YouTube clip of Kelly Starrett, a movement specialist from the USA, https://www.youtube.com/watch?v=UCF0T6t_1AU. Kelly demonstrates how to improve the compression of the rowing stroke by working specifically on the hip, hamstring and ankle with double Olympic Gold Medallist Erin Cafaro from the US Women's 8+. This is an excellent example of how to quickly improve movement quality as part of a warm-up to aid rowing technical competency.

Specific flexibility for rowing

Being flexible allows the rower to move with freedom and enables him to get more effectively into an efficient and strong position. Some key areas stiffen up when doing the miles involved in rowing training. They are the hamstrings, hip flexors, thoracic spine and shoulders. Stretching should be an integral part of the rower's training programme at the start and end of the training sessions. Specific ergometer stretching exercises can be included in the rower's conditioning circuit work.

1. Rockover stretch with a band forward on the ergometer
2. Rockover stretch with a band holding the rower back on the ergometer
3. Rockover stretch with a wobble cushion and band
4. Seated gym ball to catch in a sculling position
5. Seated gym ball to catch in a sweep position

Fig. 8.8: Rockover stretch with band from the front. This exercise is a good stretching exercise for the hamstrings that also helps develop back extensor muscles.

Mobility and Flexibility

Fig. 8.9: Rockover stretch with band from the back. This is also good for the hamstrings and helps develop local deep abdominal muscles.

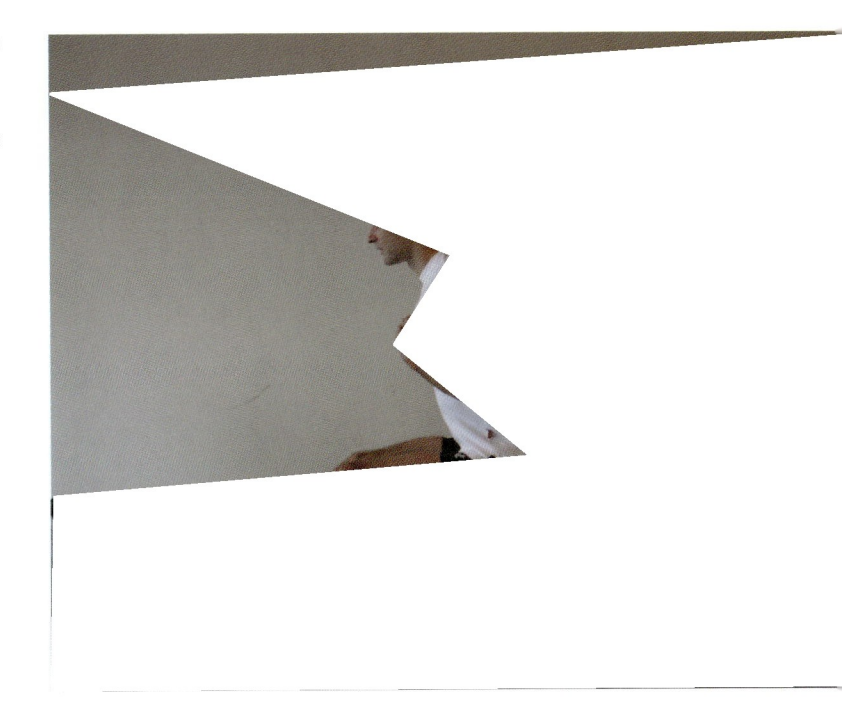

Fig. 8.10: Wobble cushion on ergometer. By sitting on a wobble cushion the rower's balance is challenged and so is his trunk control; this allows him to develop his stabilizing muscles.

Mobility and Flexibility

Fig. 8.11: Sculling Swiss ball catch. This exercise is a good stretching exercise for the latissimus dorsi muscles and also allows the rower to practise his timing between his feet and his hands at the catch, while having his balance challenged by the Swiss ball.

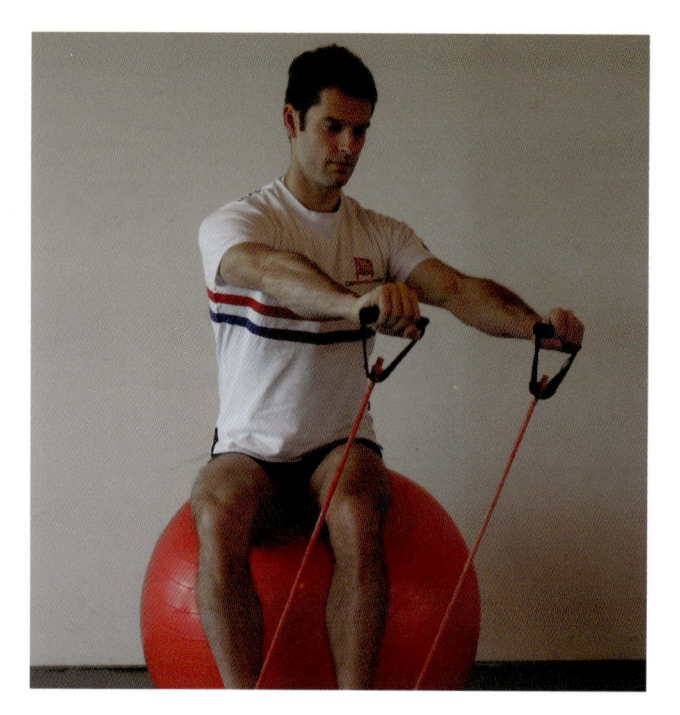

Fig. 8.12: Sweep Swiss ball catch. This exercise is also a good stretching exercise for the lattisimus dorsi but with the rotational aspect also allows good stretching through the thoracic spine. The rower will also have his balance challenged and can work on his hand to feet timing.

CHAPTER 9

WEIGHTLIFTING TECHNIQUE

Power clean

Gym health and safety

- Understand how to fail safely – there is no need for spotters.
- Ensure the lifting area is free from obstacles such as unused plate weights and gym equipment.
- Full-size bumper weights should be used when lifting from the floor; anything smaller in diameter will increase stress on the lower back.

Set-up
- Step up to the bar with the bar sitting over the toes, feet around hip width apart – each rower will have a slightly different set-up which optimizes his power clean performance.
- Take an overhand or hook grip over the bar – the grip should be wide enough to be outside of the leg. Ensure the rower grips the bar and does not allow the bar to hang from the fingers.
- The arms should be fully extended with shoulders directly over the bar.
- The hips should be slightly higher than the knees with the back maintaining a neutral position throughout.
- Take a deep breath in and hold.
- Create tension through the body by pulling slightly against the bar without the bar lifting off the floor.
- The weight should be mid-foot to heel.

Fig. 9.1: Set-up.

Weightlifting Technique

Fig. 9.2: First pull.

First pull
- Shoulders remain over or in front of the bar.
- Movement occurs as a consequence of knee extension, therefore the back angle in relation to the floor remains the same as in the start position.
- Bar path is upwards and backwards towards the rower in a controlled manner.
- The spine remains in a neutral position throughout.
- Weight distribution moves backwards towards the heel.
- First pull ends with bar hanging with straight arms slightly above and slightly in front of kneecaps.

Weightlifting Technique

Fig. 9.3: Transition.

Transition

- The knees begin to flex and move forwards under the bar with the hips extending, bringing the trunk upright and the shoulders directly above the bar.
- The spine remains in a neutral position throughout.
- The bar continues to move in an upward direction.
- Body weight moves from the heels, forward to the mid-foot to become evenly distributed.
- The arms remain straight throughout.
- The transition ends with the bar at mid-thigh and feet flat on the floor.

Weightlifting Technique

Fig. 9.4: Second pull.

Second pull

- This phase starts with the feet flat on the floor with the bar at mid- to upper thigh.
- The knees and hips are slightly flexed with shoulders directly above the bar.
- An aggressive extension of the hips, knees and ankles (triple extension) occurs, followed by a power shrug of the shoulders.
- The bar will make contact with the upper thigh due to the aggressive triple extension.
- Weight acts through the centre of the foot as force for the triple extension is applied.
- Bar remains close to the body and continues in an upward direction with arms straight until the triple extension and shoulder shrug is complete.
- The second pull ends with a fully extended body, bar at top of thigh and the shoulders shrugged.

Weightlifting Technique

Fig. 9.5: Catch.

The catch

- The elbows break and start to bend due to the momentum of the bar.
- The elbows flex outwardly, parallel to the line of the bar – once the bar is about to be caught, the elbows rotate under the bar in a rapid action.
- The feet 'jump' outwards to a near squat foot position.
- The body weight is mid-foot to heel of the foot.
- The hips, knees and ankles simultaneously flex to drop beneath the bar – the entire body 'stiffens' to catch the bar and stop the bar driving the body into a deep squat position.
- The bar is caught in a front squat position, the rower loosens his grip on the bar as it rests across the anterior shoulders – hands should not be caught between the bar and the shoulders.
- The elbows are pointing forward to create the shelf for the bar to rest on the shoulders.
- The trunk remains in an upright position with a neutral spinal position maintained.

Common faults

Hips rise first at the ascent
Technical cue: Reduce the load. Hips and chest rise at the same rate. Initiate ascent by driving heels into the floor. Ensure the hips are set lower than the shoulders at the start.

Coaching cue: Lead with the chest ('big chest'), drive upwards through the heels.

95

Weightlifting Technique

Arm swing
Technical point: Where is the body during the transition phase? Hips usually rising early (see point above). Elbows break along the line of the bar at end of second pull.

Coaching cues: Instruct the rower to pull the bar into the body. Keep the shoulders over the bar for longer. 'Elbow target above shoulders'.

Single pull from floor
Technical point: No transition phase or repositioning of knees and hips in second pull. With submaximal loading, develop the technical positions from first pull, transition and second pull.

Coaching cues: Control load of bar from floor to knee, explode when the bar is above the knee.

Back squat

Gym health and safety
- Understanding how to squat safely with and without spotters is essential, including how to fail a lift safely.
- Pay careful attention to how each squat rack can be adjusted to de-rack and rack the bar safely and effectively and how to adjust the safety bars to the correct height for the depth of the squat.
- Ensure the lifting area is free from obstacles such as unused plate weights and gym equipment.

Set-up
- Set the bar to the height of the armpit of the squatter.
- Stand at arm's length away from the bar, taking a grip wider than the shoulders – use the markings on the bar to ensure symmetry of hand position.
- Step under the centre of the bar with feet directly under the bar.
- Create a 'shelf' for the bar to rest on by drawing back the shoulder blades.
- The bar should rest on the fleshy 'shelf' and not the bony protrusions of the neck – maintain this position throughout the lift.
- Take a deep breath and hold.
- Lift the bar from the rack and take a small step backwards to clear the rack.

Fig. 9.6: Start and finish position of the back squat.

Weightlifting Technique

Fig. 9.7: Bottom of the descent of the back squat.

- Adjust feet to between hip and slightly greater than shoulder width with toes pointing at 11 (left) and 1 (right) on the clock face – each rower will have a slightly different set-up which optimizes his squat performance.
- Body weight is mid-foot before descending.

Descent

- Take a deep breath in and hold throughout the lift until returning close to the top of the ascent. This will help to maintain a neutral spine throughout the movement.
- Under control, simultaneously flex the hips and knees so that the hips move backwards past the heels of the feet. Correct squat depth is top of hips parallel with the knees.
- The spine must maintain a neutral position with no rounding of the upper back (thoracic spine) or flattening of the lower back (lumbar spine).
- The body weight will move from mid-foot to heel during the descent.
- The hip, knee and ankle alignment should be maintained throughout – a common fault is knees tracking towards each other.
- The angle of the trunk and shin in relation to the floor should be fairly similar to each other.

Ascent

- Aggressively return the bar to the start by forcibly driving the heels into the floor.
- The hips and shoulders should rise simultaneously at the same speed, with the spine maintaining its neutral position.
- The weight moves from heel to mid-foot towards the top of the ascent.
- Exhale from previous deep breath and inhale again in preparation for the next repetition.

Re-racking

- Walk forward into the rack until hearing both the left and right side make contact with the rack.
- Squat the bar back into the rack – don't lean forward to rack the bar as this can increase the risk of injury.

Common faults

Hips rise first at the ascent
Technical cue: Reduce the load. Hips and chest rise at the same rate. Initiate ascent by driving heels into the floor.

Coaching cue: Lead with the chest, drive upwards through the heels.

Weightlifting Technique

Knee valgus (knees coming together)
Technical cue: Reduce the load. Maintain lumbar neutral and thoracic extension. Scapula set back and down.

Coaching cue: Drive the knees outwards away from each other. Adjust width of the feet and the toes' position to optimize the knee alignment.

Flexed spine during the descent and ascent
Technical cue: Lower the load. Maintain lumbar neutral and thoracic extension. Scapula set back and down.

Coaching cues: 'Big chest'. Instruct the rower to 'squeeze an orange between his shoulder blades'.

Squatting through the toes (not heel)
Technical points: Weight moves to the rear foot during the descent. Sit back into the squat, leading with the hips. Flat foot throughout.

Coaching cues: 'Hips back'/'sit back' into the bottom position.

Back squat spotting

It is important when lifting near maximal loads that there is a 'spotter'. A spotter is a training partner or coach who ensures the safety of the lifting. The spotter will help lift the bar from the rack and help safely return it once the desired repetitions are finished. The spotter will also help reduce the risk of injury if the rower fails a repetition. If a rower is failing, the spotter will help lift the bar and aid the safe return to the rack. During the back squat, a single spotter may stand behind the rower. He may guide the rower out of the cage as he takes a step backwards to clear the rack. Once the rower has completed the desired number of repetitions, the spotter may take a grip on the bar and help return the bar to the rack. It is important that both the spotter and rower have excellent communication. When the spotter helps lift the bar from the rack, the rower should inform the spotter to release the bar by saying 'my bar' when ready to squat. This will prompt the spotter to release his grip and allow the rower to start squatting. When the rower has finished his set, the spotter will once again grip the bar and inform the rower he has control of the bar by saying 'my bar'. This will inform the rower that the spotter has control and is guiding the bar back to the rack. A three-man spotting technique can also be used, with one spotter at either end of the bar and one behind the rower. This technique is often used with heavy loads or when a single spotter may not feel comfortable to assist on his own.

Deadlift

Gym health and safety

- Understand how to fail safely – there is no need for spotters.
- Ensure the lifting area is free from obstacles such as unused plate weights and gym equipment.
- Full-size bumper weights should be used when lifting from the floor; anything smaller in diameter will increase stress on the lower back.

Set-up

- Step up to the bar with the bar sitting over the toes, feet around hip width apart – each rower will have a slightly different set-up which optimizes his deadlift performance.
- Take an overhand grip over the bar – the grip should be wide enough to be outside of the leg. Ensure the rower grips the bar and does not allow the bar to hang from the fingers.

Weightlifting Technique

Fig. 9.8: Start position for the deadlift.

- The arms should be fully extended with shoulders directly over the bar.
- The hips should be slightly higher than the knees, with the back maintaining a neutral position throughout.
- Take a deep breath in and hold.
- Create tension through the body by pulling slightly against the bar without the bar lifting off the floor.
- The weight should be mid-foot to heel.

Ascent
- Initiate the movement by driving the feet into the floor.
- The hips and shoulders should rise simultaneously at the same speed with the spine maintaining its neutral position.
- Shoulders remain over the bar until the bar passes the knees – as the bar passes the knees the trunk becomes upright using an aggressive hip extension.
- The weight moves from heel to mid-foot towards the top of the ascent.
- The bar should move in an up and slightly backwards direction and be in near contact with the body at all times.
- At the top of the ascent, exhale.

Descent
- There are physiological adaptation benefits to returning the bar to the floor for the posterior chain (gluteals and hamstrings) but only with submaximal loads.
- Complete the ascent in reverse with a slight rockover from the hips first, lowering the bar to just above the knees.
- Control the bar to the floor.
- Alternatively, drop the bar from the top of the ascent.

Fig. 9.9: Top of ascent of the deadlift.

Weightlifting Technique

Common faults

Flexed spine
Technical points: Lower the load. Place pre-tension on the bar, i.e. 'know the load'. Scapula set back and down. Controlled, patient lift off the floor.

Coaching cues: Take the slack out of the arms. Instruct the rower to tighten his back. Don't attempt to lift the bar off the floor at full speed. Be patient. Instruct the rower to have a 'big chest'. Lead with the chest.

Hips rise first at the ascent
Technical cue: Reduce the load. Hips and chest rise at the same rate. Initiate ascent by driving heels into the floor. Ensure the hips are set lower than the shoulders at the start.

Coaching cue: Lead with the chest ('big chest'), drive upwards through the heels.

Bar drifts away from the body/shoulder not over the bar
Technical point: Where is the body during the transition phase? Hips usually rising early (see point above).

Coaching cues: Instruct the rower to pull the bar into the body. Keep the shoulders over the bar for longer.

Knee valgus
Technical cue: Reduce the load. Maintain lumbar neutral and thoracic extension. Scapula set back and down.

Coaching cue: Drive the knees outwards away from each other. Adjust width of the feet and the toes' position to optimize the knee alignment.

Bench press

Gym health and safety
- Understanding how to bench press safely with and without spotters is essential, including how to fail a lift safely.
- Pay careful attention to how each bench press can be adjusted to de-rack and rack the bar safely.
- Ensure the lifting area is free from obstacles such as unused plate weights and gym equipment.

Set-up
- Lie on the bench ensuring the head is supported by the bench – the eye line should be in line with the bar.
- Ensure the feet are in contact with the floor – if unable to safely or comfortably have the feet in contact with the floor, use a box or plate weights to place the feet on.
- Foot position should be either directly under the knees or slightly closer to the hips.
- Take a symmetrical grip slightly wider than shoulder width with a closed grip – each rower will have a slightly different set-up which optimizes their bench press performance.
- Grip the bench with shoulder blades (back and down).
- Press the bar out of the rack and bring the bar to a position so that the arms are totally vertical.

Descent
- Take a deep breath and hold throughout the lift.
- In a controlled manner, lower the bar to the chest, roughly 2–3cm from the bottom of the sternum.
- Allow the elbows to drift slightly inwards towards the torso – this should feel like attempting to 'bend' the bar.

Weightlifting Technique

Fig. 9.10: Bottom of descent of the bench press.

Fig. 9.11: Top of ascent of the bench press.

- The head, shoulders, hips and feet should remain in contact with the bench or floor respectively.

Ascent
- Aggressively return the bar to the start by forcibly driving shoulders through the bench and feet through the floor.
- Drive the bar to the ceiling in an upward and slightly backward direction so the arms return to a vertical position.
- The head, shoulders, hips and feet should remain in contact with the bench or floor respectively.
- Exhale from previous deep breath and inhale again in preparation for the next repetition.

Re-racking
- In a controlled manner, slowly return the bar to the rack until hearing contact of the bar with the left and right rack.
- Slowly lower the bar into the rack.

Common faults

Bar not touching chest
Technical cue: Reduce the load. Adjust hand position to allow full elbow flexion. Practise technique of bringing elbows inwards to the torso during the descent.

Coaching cue: 'Bend the bar'.

Bar placement on chest too high
Technical cue: Reduce the load. Practise bringing the bar to just below the nipple line. Width of grip may need to be adjusted.

Coaching cue: Lower bar to chest, not to neck.

Grip width
Technical cue: Too wide a grip creates excessive stress on shoulders and elbows, too narrow increases triceps contribution. Adjust grip to slightly wider than shoulder width.

Weightlifting Technique

Coaching cue: Without a bar and lying on back, extend arms upwards. Note distance between hands – this is a rough guide for grip width.

Back squat spotting

During the bench press, the spotter will stand behind the bench (at the end of the bench where the rower's head is supported), with the bar between the spotter and rower. The spotter will help lift the bar from the rack and help safely return it once the desired repetitions are finished. The spotter will also help reduce the risk of injury if the rower fails a repetition. If a rower is failing, the spotter will help lift the bar and aid the safe return to the rack. It is important that both the spotter and rower have excellent communication. When the spotter helps lift the bar from the rack, the rower should inform the spotter to release the bar by saying 'my bar' when ready to lift. This will prompt the spotter to release his grip and allow the rower to start lifting. When the rower has finished his set, the spotter will once again grip the bar and inform the rower he has control of the bar by saying 'my bar'. This will inform the rower that the spotter has control and is guiding the bar back to the rack. It is, however, important to note that the rower should not release his grip of the bar until the bar is safely returned.

Bench pull

Gym health and safety

- Understanding how to bench pull safely is essential, including how to fail a lift safely.
- Pay careful attention to how each bench pull can be adjusted to de-rack and rack the bar safely.
- Ensure the lifting area is free from obstacles such as unused plate weights and gym equipment.

Fig. 9.12: Set-up and finish position of the bench pull.

Set-up

- Lie on the bench face down ensuring your head is supported by the bench or sits within the face hole provided on some benches.
- To reduce the amount of lumbar flexion and extension while executing the exercise, it is ideal to straddle the bench with a leg either side with around a 90° hip flexion.
- If this is not possible, use a partner to fix the legs to the bench; legs that are not fixed cause a great lumbar extension by the legs flailing in the air (like a fish tail).
- Take a grip of the bar that is wider than the width of the bench pull itself with an overhand grip.
- Once the bar is taken from the rack, the bar should hang perpendicular to the floor with arms long.
- Set the shoulders by 'squeezing' the shoulder blades back and down while simultaneously 'bracing the trunk'.

Weightlifting Technique

Fig. 9.13: Top of the ascent for the bench pull.

Ascent
- Take a deep breath and hold throughout the ascent.
- In a forceful manner, pull the bar to the bench, roughly in line with the bottom of the sternum; the bar should move in a vertical upward manner with no swinging of the bar.
- The elbows should be pulled toward the trunk of the rower and not outwards.
- The bar should make contact with the underside of the bench; benches have different depths but the recommended depth is 5–7cm; any less, rowers will hyperextend their back to gain the extra range, any more, the rower loses the strength benefits of the exercise.
- The head, chest and the trunk must remain on the bench throughout the ascent.

Descent
- In a controlled manner return the bar to the start position by allowing the elbows to extend. Don't let the bar drop in an uncontrolled manner.
- The bar should be returned so that the arms are long and perpendicular to the floor.
- The head, chest and trunk should remain in contact with the bench throughout the descent.
- Exhale from previous deep breath when the bar is returned and inhale again in preparation for the next repetition.

Re-racking
- In a controlled manner, slowly return the bar to the rack until you hear contact of the bar with the rack.
- Slowly lower the bar into the rack.

Common faults

Bar not touching underside of bench
Technical cue: Reduce the load. Practise technique of bringing elbows inwards to the torso during the ascent.

Coaching cue: 'Bend the bar'.

Bar pulled to upper chest and not to bottom of sternum
Technical cue: Reduce the load. Practise technique of bringing elbows inwards to the torso during the ascent.

Coaching cue: 'Bend the bar'.

Hyper extension of back
Technical cue: Reduce the load. Rower to maintain 'braced' trunk.

Coaching cue: Grip the bench with legs/anchor legs with partner holding legs in place.

CHAPTER 10

TRUNK

Before talking about trunk training for rowing, it is important to define what we mean by the term 'trunk' and its training purpose. Fundamentally, there are two training focuses for the trunk. The first is to ensure the integrity of the spine and its associated soft tissues and to reduce the risk of spinal injury. The second is to develop the ability of the trunk to help improve performance.

The terms trunk and core have been used interchangeably throughout the last decade to describe the body part, yet they can be interpreted as two different components of the same body segment. In essence, when someone is using the term trunk it refers to everything from the shoulder girdle down to the pelvic and hip girdle. The trunk can be defined as the global system. It consists of the superficial muscles that span many joint segments. They are direction-specific (the direction is dictated by the orientation of the muscle fibres) and fatigue rapidly. These muscles form a muscular corset between the ribcage, spine and pelvic girdle and work together to control spinal position. The muscle cross-sectional area is larger when compared to the local system (defined below) and therefore has a greater force application capability.

As described in Chapter 6, rowing is a whole body action where there needs to be transfer of force from the leg drive, through the trunk and on to the handles of the oar. To gain some insight into the importance of the trunk, the contribution of the trunk towards the force output of the rowing stroke is around 31 per cent (Kleshnev, 1991). The trunk is working at around 55 per cent of its maximal capacity (Kleshnev, 1991), suggesting that the trunk's involvement during the stroke is submaximal but is consistently active throughout the stroke. This gives coaches a greater understanding of how the trunk can potentially be trained to optimize performance and reduce the risk of injury. Chapter 2 identified that for a rower to move into the appropriate position to optimize the rockover, there is a balance between having long, flexible lats and hip flexors while having a strong trunk to maintain spinal position. A strong and stable trunk will allow for optimal force transfer from legs to arms to oars. A weak trunk leaks energy and costs the rower boat speed, as not all the energy generated from the leg drive is transferred to the oars.

Force application with regard to movement can be broken down into three areas, as highlighted in Fig. 10.1. The first type of force application is generation, where the trunk can rotate, flex and extend, and laterally flex and extend. Force transfer is the ability of the trunk to transmit or amplify the force moving from lower body to upper body or vice versa, posterior to anterior or vice versa, medially to laterally or vice versa. Force control refers to the trunk's ability for postural control and resisting deformation due to external and internal loads (i.e. the body's ability to exert forces onto the trunk, such as the leg drive from catch to maximal handle load).

It becomes important when we define trunk training for the rower to recognize the

Trunk

Fig. 10.1: Force application during movement.

Force Generation	Force Transfer	Force Control
Rotation	Proximal to distal (vice versa)	Postural control
Block Rotation	Lower body to upper body (vice versa)	Resist deformation from external loads
Flexion / Extension	Posterior to anterior (vice versa)	Resist deformation from internal loads
Lateral Flexion / Extension	Medial to lateral (vice versa)	

trunk's function in force application. From Fig. 10.1 it is clear that the trunk has an ability to contribute to an athletic action through generating force itself, transferring force from limb to limb and maintaining effective posture for that athletic action. Interestingly, in the majority of the trunk muscles, with the exception of the rectus abdominus, transverse abdominus and spinalis portions of the spinal erectors, the superficial muscles are orientated in an oblique fashion. This oblique orientation allows the trunk to generate or transfer force while also controlling against exerting forces that may disturb the trunk's optimal position. Few athletic actions occur in a single plane of movement, particularly within sweep rowing, as the athletic movements are three-dimensional and require a rotational component. In sculling, the athletic actions involve resisting a rotational force, such as when a rower is at the catch, where the boat may be slightly unbalanced, as may also be the case when rowing in a crosswind.

Examples of the global muscles of the trunk can be found in Fig. 10.2. The trunk is more commonly aligned with performance outcomes due to the architecture and force-producing capability of the superficial muscles. However, the ability of these muscles to dissipate large forces before they are transmitted to the spine is also important to consider; therefore, the musculature can also be defined as important in reducing the risk of injury to the spine.

In contrast, the local system is typically called the core. These muscles are deeper, smaller, non-direction specific, and have a high resistance to fatigue. While the global muscles create spinal movement, these smaller core muscles stabilize the spine at segmental level (vertebrae and discs). What is unique around these muscles is their anticipatory activity, which allows a feed-forward approach where the muscles can anticipate instability. For example, if you are standing on a bus without holding on for stability, when the bus pulls away you feel unstable; however, these core muscles will stabilize the spine in anticipation of the instability prior to you regaining full stability. For these reasons, the core muscles are unable to be the primary force-producing driver for sporting actions, which is the role of the global superficial muscles. Examples of the local core muscles can be found in Fig. 10.2. These muscles are orientated closer to the spine, allowing for the segmental control.

Core stability is spinal segmental control. Spinal segmental control is the body's ability to maintain one vertebra on top of the other in a uniform and optimal fashion while completing anything from everyday tasks through to high performance rowing. The term 'core stability' is frequently misused in describing unstable training where the rower uses equipment such as Swiss balls or BOSU balls. The rower is placed in an unstable environment in which he attempts to create stability with the idea that this will improve core stability. While unstable surface training can assist in core stability training, it

Trunk

Local Trunk Muscles (core)	Global Trunk Muscles
Diaphragm	Rectus Abdominals (RA)
Transverse Abdominals (TVA)	External Obliques (EO)
Pelvic Floor	Internal Obliques (IO)
Multifidus	Superficial fibres of Erector Spinae
Lower fibres of Internal Obliques	Lateral fibres of Quadratus Lumborum
Deep fibres of Psoas	Illiacus
Deep fibres of Erector Spinae	Superficial fibres of Psoas
Medial fibres of Quadratus Lumborum (QL)	Rectus Femoris
	Adductors
	Gluteals
	Hamstrings
	Piriformis

Fig. 10.2: Local and global muscles of the trunk.

should not be used as the only modality, as there is evidence to suggest that the greater the instability the rower is facing, the greater the requirement from the superficial global system to stabilize the spine. This defeats the object of the initial intention to develop the control and coordination of the deeper muscles surrounding the spine. When faced with an unstable surface, the body will try to create rigidity or stiffness to protect the spine from buckling or being exposed to unnecessary forces. An untrained rower will automatically create the necessary stiffness by contracting the majority of muscles under unstable conditions, which ultimately reduces range of movement, which in turn impacts on the appropriate movement mechanics. With more training, the rower is able to coordinate muscular contractions, allowing the more superficial muscles to become less active while completing a dynamic task as the deeper muscles surrounding the spine take a greater role in spinal stability.

This process is often seen when a novice rower takes to the water for the first time. The rower is unable to get into the desired position straight away as he is trying to create stability to stop himself falling out of the boat. The rower is likely to have a shortened stroke length both at the front and back end and may not even be able to get into a full rockover. As the rower progresses and becomes more accustomed to rowing on water, he is able to start coordinating movement more effectively, requiring less of the bigger superficial muscles for stability, which then allows him to start increasing the range of movement around joints. At this point, the rower begins to increase the range of movement during the rowing stroke and starts to look more like the rowing technical model.

Commonly, with lower back pain sufferers, a large amount of attention is focused upon core training, including core stability as defined above. The intention is to improve spinal control, with the assumption that with greater control there is an associated reduction in back pain. This is correct; however, with lower back pain and associated injuries, trunk training as defined above must be considered and included to improve total spinal function and control.

Neither the trunk nor the core can work in isolation and recognition of the importance of both in health and in performance is necessary. A bias towards one over the other can lead to greater dysfunction and pain. However, those rowers who have good core control and stability do not need to spend as much time on this type of training because it is a skill and not a physical quality, i.e. the ability to learn to stabilize the spine has a larger neurological bias to its training over high force trunk training, where morphological changes may be necessary.

Trunk training

Fig. 10.3 defines the volume and intensity of different training modalities for the trunk. The hierarchy is based on the intensity and volume of each modality and the specificity to athletic performance. It is not based on a didactic model of having to complete the base layer before moving onto the layer above and it is not hierarchical in terms of the most important training modality being at the top. The greater the intensity of training, the lower the volume of this type of work can be completed. The training guidelines for the trunk are similar to those of the strength training paradigm discussed in Chapter 6. For example, the physiological principles of adaptation are the same, therefore maximal strength or high force training is achieved in the same way as if the rower is maximally strength-training his legs. The greatest difference is when looking at optimally training the core (local system).

Core training

Core training has been described as core stability, motor recruitment, motor control or activation training. They are all terms that are synonymous with one another, with the training outcome being very similar, if not the same. Core training is the first layer within Fig. 10.3 (trunk training hierarchy). This type of training is often used to train or retrain the motor control aspect of spinal segments.

It is important that the intensity of training is low (less than 30 per cent of 1RM equivalent). The focus must be on the technical execution of the skill or movement over the load in which it is being used. If technique starts to break down, either the load or the volume is

Fig. 10.3: Hierarchy of trunk training based on intensity and volume.

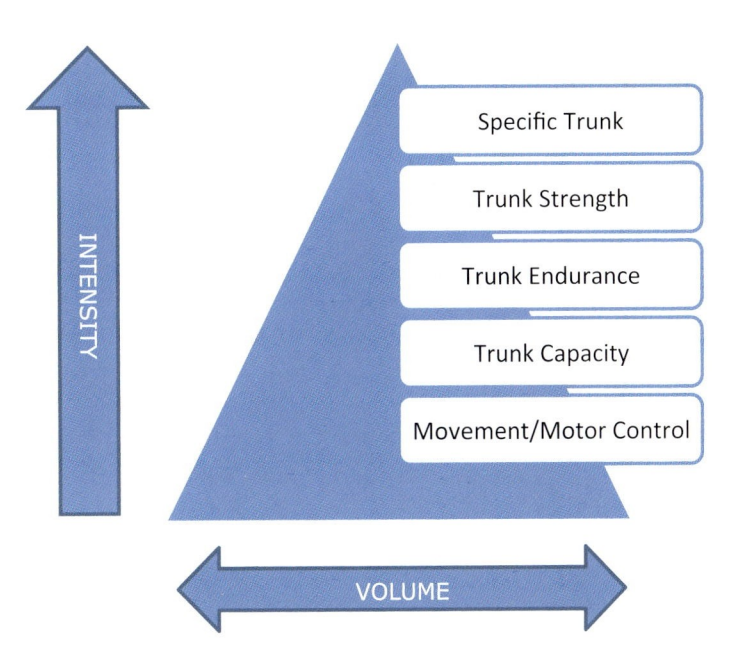

Trunk

greater than that which the rower is capable of sustaining. While some fatigue is necessary, it cannot compromise technique. The mass of the rower's limbs is generally enough to challenge him, while also creating enough of a stimulus for adaptation. The volume of training can be quite high, with 3–5 sets of 20 or more repetitions, or, if maintaining a static (isometric) contraction, around 30–60 seconds of work. Due to the low energy cost of this type of training, a rower is able to complete the training more than 3 times a week, as much as daily or even 2–3 times a day. It is very important to work with a skilled practitioner in prescribing and correcting technique for core training exercises. While the rower may seem to be completing the exercise correctly, the skilled practitioner will be able to ascertain if the movement quality is actually correct. As with all coaching tasks, the more practice done, the better the understanding of the technical model and the physical requirements necessary for the exercise becomes. If this area is new, work closely with physiotherapists and strength and conditioning coaches not only to ensure the rower is performing the exercise correctly but also to help develop your understanding and application of these types of exercises.

Once a rower is able to complete the core training exercises with high proficiency, the need to continue them in the same volume is reduced. While all the trunk training is effectively learning a skill, core training requires fewer physical qualities when compared to strength endurance or strength. Once the rower has become skilful at the tasks, a minimal programme of core exercises can be completed to maintain the movement qualities that have been developed. However, it is important to note that it can take a rower a long time to master the movements and become highly proficient at them, so it can be a significant part of the rower's training programme. This is more evident with rowers who are returning to training after an episode of lower back pain.

Pain is exceptionally good at disrupting clean movement patterns and creating confusion around the coordination of previously well-rehearsed and effective movement control of the spine. It cannot be stressed enough that when a rower has had an episode of lower back pain, before any type of training is completed the rower must be pain-free. If the rower is not, the learning and execution of the core training exercises are significantly compromised. The body will find any way it can to complete the task, which may not be the most efficient or effective for the spine but the only way it can complete it due to the presence of pain. Once pain is removed, the rower will have to relearn the core training movement as the body will have a faulty pattern ingrained and will continue to complete the task in the same manner as when it was originally in pain, even though the pain has been removed. This type of training is heavily used post-lower back injury and pain, as it helps the rower to relearn the movement patterns which are important to spinal segmental control.

Trunk endurance

Trunk endurance is the second training focus within Fig. 10.3. As described earlier in this chapter, the trunk has been shown to contribute 31 per cent of the total work a rower needs to complete each stroke, and works submaximally throughout the stoke (Kleshnev, 1991). This is an important consideration when looking at trunk training for the rower. While attention has been given to core training, this section is the closest to rowing performance in terms of duration of the exercise prescription (2–10 minutes) and the submaximal intensity, which is closer to the demands of the trunk during a 2,000m event. When compared

Trunk

Fig. 10.4: Trunk endurance training programme.

Exercise	Quadrant	Sets x Time
Front Plank	Anterior	2 x 30 seconds
Partner Resisted Left Plank	Left	2 x 30 seconds
Back Extension	Posterior	2 x 30 seconds
Partner Resisted Right Plank	Right	2 x 30 seconds
Swiss Ball Rollout	Anterior	2 x 30 seconds

* Complete one set of each exercise and move to the next exercise in the list. After finishing one set of each, complete the final set of each exercise in order

to the strength training paradigm (Fig. 6.3 in Chapter 6), trunk endurance training is closer in its nature to strength condition training or hypertrophy training in terms of the exercise prescription. The intensity should be between 60–80 per cent of 1RM or its equivalent and the activity should be hard to maximal. Typical volume would be 3–5 sets of 5–10 repetitions or, if completing static (isometric) exercises, 30–60 seconds. There is a high energy cost and physical demand to this type of training, therefore it should be completed at maximum 2–3 times a week, with at least 48 hours' recovery between sessions. It is necessary to fatigue the rower throughout the training.

Fig. 10.4 outlines a fundamental trunk endurance training programme that is typical for a rower. Attention should be drawn to a number of points. Firstly, because this is trunk endurance, there is very little or no recovery between each exercise set. Normally, the time taken to move from one exercise to the next is all the recovery that a rower is given. Secondly, to ensure the rower can maintain a higher intensity of loading throughout the training programme for each exercise, exercises are organized so that the same quadrant is not trained consecutively. For example, if a front plank is completed, which is an anterior trunk-dominant exercise, the next exercise completed will be one from the three remaining quadrants (left lateral, right lateral or posterior back). This pattern continues whereby exercises focusing on different trunk quadrants follow each other.

Fig. 10.5: Front plank.

Trunk

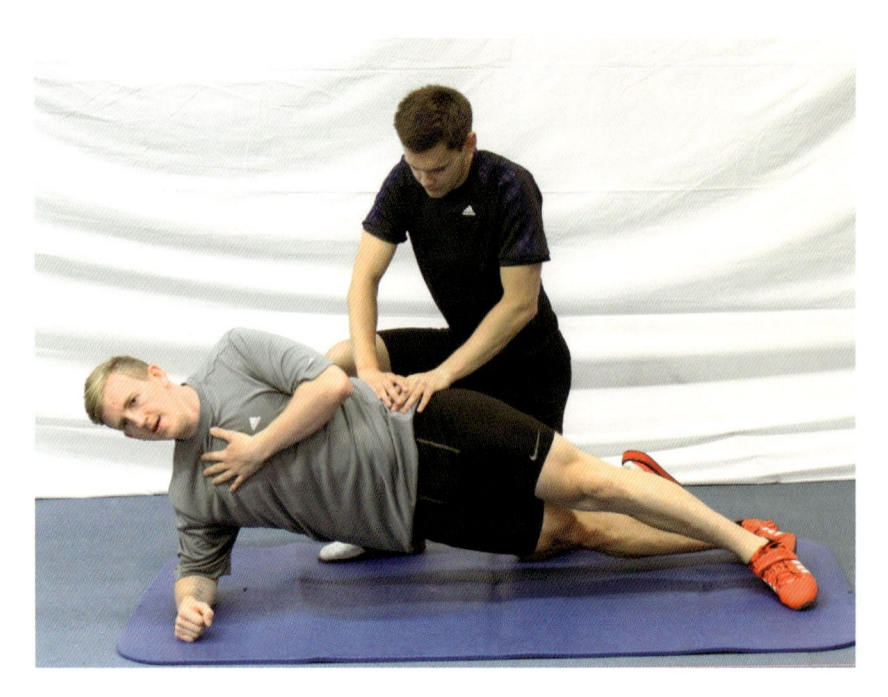

Fig. 10.6: Partner-resisted right plank.

Fig. 10.7: Loaded back extension.

Fig. 10.8: Swiss ball rollout.

Trunk strength

Chapter 6 describes the impact of strong (forceful) muscles on economy of endurance performance by increasing the maximal capability. Trunk strength training is an excellent way to increase the trunk's maximal capacity. Maximal strength capacity through the trunk is also important at the start of the race or when there are sudden and aggressive changes in stroke rate while rowing. At the start of the race, the rower takes his first stroke from a dead start, so there are very large forces going through the entire body including the trunk during the first few strokes. When there is a sudden increase in stroke rate, a similar effect is seen on the trunk, where there is an increase in the forces the trunk has to tolerate. The trunk not only needs a submaximal capacity that will tolerate loading throughout the race, it also needs to be able to deal with greater forces that may occur at any point in the race. It is important to note that every time the blade enters the water at the catch, there is a spike in the load the rower experiences, which again increases the forces going through the trunk. Therefore the function of the trunk requires the ability to sustain a submaximal capacity throughout each stroke, while also being able to work maximally when the trunk is under greater load at the start of the stroke, firstly to reduce the risk of injury and secondly to improve the rower's performance.

Trunk strength training requires a high force stimulus where the rower has to work at greater than 80 per cent of 1RM or its equivalent. The training needs to be hard to maximal, with common volumes being 3–6 sets of 1–6 repetitions, or 5–8 seconds of static holds. This type of training can be completed 1–3 times a week. Fatigue is not necessary, but the rower must train with intent (see Chapter 6) to benefit from the full training adaptation. When identifying the exercises to use to develop trunk strength, based on the philosophy of training the adaptation and not the exercise, as long as the loading strategies follow the guidelines above, the same exercises in Figs 10.5–10.8 can be used. For instance, increasing the resistance during the partner-resisted side planks (Fig. 10.6) simply requires the partner to create more resistance by pushing harder downwards onto the rower's hips. Fig. 10.9 is an example of a trunk strength training programme using the same exercises as identified above.

Trunk

Fig. 10.9: Trunk strength training programme.

Exercise	Quadrant	Sets x Reps
Partner Resisted Front Plank	Anterior	3 x 10 (2 second hold)*
Partner Resisted Left Plank	Left	2 x 10 (2 second hold)*
Back Extension	Posterior	3 x 10
Partner Resisted Right Plank	Right	2 x 10 (2 second hold)*

* One repetition is two seconds of partner resistance

Coxswain training

It is relevant to discuss the training of coxswains in this chapter, as trunk training is probably the area in which coxswains can make the biggest physical impact to enhance boat speed, while maintaining aerobic fitness and managing body composition.

Although the significant majority of the physical exertion in a boat is performed by rowers, there is a need for the coxswain to have a fundamental level of fitness for a number of reasons. The demands of being a coxswain are more than simply leading a group of rowers charging towards the finish line in a regatta. Their role can be varied during training, whether in the boat or out. Coxswains may help with some of the coaching and at times be cycling along the river or lake edge. The bigger the boat, the faster the speed, so having a fundamental level of aerobic fitness is important.

A stronger case for fundamental levels of aerobic fitness (and good nutritional habits) is around body composition. Olympic-class men's and women's coxed boats have to carry the mass of the coxswain. Excessive body fat, whether on a rower or a coxswain, has the potential to reduce boat speed. Body fat is also an uncontrollable soft tissue, unlike muscle which can be contracted to create stiffness or rigidity. A lean coxswain will have greater control of his entire body mass, and can therefore create a better streamlined position and make movements in the boat that cost less boat speed. While boat speeds are not as great as in, for example, track cycling team pursuit, where streamlined positions are critical to reducing the impact of drag on bike speed, an unstable coxswain can disrupt the boat and equally reduce boat speed. Chapters 3–5 are geared towards training a rower's performance, but the sessions outlined in those chapters are also useful for the coxswain to increase his aerobic fitness and help manage body composition, alongside a healthy diet (Chapter 11). The training can be completed as other modalities such as running, cycling, cross-training or circuit training. There is no limit to what type or how a coxswain's aerobic training can be organized.

Referring back to the streamlined position and stability of the boat, this is where trunk training can make a significant impact on the coxswain's performance. A strong and stable trunk will allow the coxswain to maintain an uncompromised body position throughout the race and will allow him to have control of his body. For example, when the coxswain is observing racing crews around him, he can maintain the trunk position and only rotate his head from the neck upwards. The trunk remains rigid so as not to compromise the boat balance with big changes in mass moving from a central to a more lateral position in the boat. Vertical displacement of the coxswain will also have an impact on boat speed. Maintaining a constant centre of mass will reduce the potential increases in vertical displacement of the boat, which can increase the drag across the hull and therefore reduce boat speed.

A concern for coxswains is the potential risk of injury to the lumbar spine due to the position held while racing. Although injuries are rare and tend not to be as severe as lumbar spine injuries to rowers, they can be equally debilitating. Coxswains will flex from the hip and spine to maintain a streamlined position. Unlike a rower, where the technical model strongly works on the hips to create the rockover position without flexing through the spine, the coxswain has no choice but to flex through the spine to create the required streamlined position. As discussed earlier in the chapter, pain can alter the control of movement and positioning. A coxswain in pain is likely to change his patterning to reduce pain sensation, which will impact on boat speed due to the lack of control and stability. Clearly the coxswain's health is of paramount interest in any case, but it is important in reducing the risk of the coxswain being a limiting factor in boat speed by ensuring he has a healthy back.

The suggestions around trunk training in this chapter are of equal merit for coxswains and rowers. A coxswain who has a strong and stable trunk will be able to tolerate the rigours of long training outings and the faster competitive pacing of racing too. Alongside trunk training, attention should also be paid to maintaining the thoracic extension range of movement (Chapter 8), as this is often lost when many hours a week are spent in a flexed spine position. For the same reason, attention should also be paid to hip extension. Range will be lost, and if the coxswain cannot gain full extension in either, this will only serve to exacerbate the impact of excessive flexion on pain and injury.

CHAPTER 11

NUTRITION

Preparation is everything in rowing performance and, while races are raced on race day, they are often won and lost on the training. The quality of training is the basis of performance. For a rower to get the most out of his training means he needs to get the most out of his body. To get the most out of his body it needs to be fuelled well. It is important to optimize adaptation from training through appropriate nutritional interventions, which in turn will aid future competitive performances. Therefore, it is important to split nutrition into two sections: training nutrition and competition nutrition.

Performance nutrition starts with food and the basics

In any rower's diet the significant majority of nutrition should come from food and the majority of this should be unprocessed, unrefined and, wherever possible, fresh. A balanced diet is imperative and should be the cornerstone of everyone's diet, whether they are a rower or the spouse or parent of a rower. Head of Nutrition at the English Institute of Sport, Kevin Currell continually reinforces this message by insisting we need to 'unleash the power of food'. At the Winston Churchill War Rooms in London, one propaganda poster reinforces how important good nutrition is by stating 'Victory is in the Kitchen'. This alone is a strong message to all athletes and one that often goes unheard. There are plenty of resources available on fulfilling a balanced and healthy diet and, for brevity, the remainder of this chapter will focus on the rower's nutritional demands during training and competition.

Training nutrition

As already identified in previous chapters, a rowing programme has a real mix of aerobic and anaerobic training, including variants of strength training. There are two areas which may present challenges to the rower during training blocks. The first is multiple training sessions per day, with the second being concurrent training, whereby the rower is trying to adapt to two competing stimuli: aerobic endurance training versus anaerobic strength training.

Multiple training sessions within a day

The previous chapters have highlighted that rowing is a high volume training sport. For a rower to develop the physiological and technical components required for racing, there are occasions where there is a need to complete two or more training sessions within a single day. For the international and high performance rower, this is a regular requirement. For club and university rowers, training twice a day may be required at particular parts of the season or within the training week. Any rower who attends a training camp, regardless of level, will be expected to train more than once a day too. Endurance training can take as long as 2 hours to complete, which will also require fuelling and hydration strategies within the training session itself. With multiple training sessions in a day and an accumulated volume through the training week, there is a need to ensure that each rower is nutritionally prepared for the session to optimize adaptation from the training stimulus and to recover adequately in preparation for the next session.

Concurrent training

As described in Chapter 6, concurrent training is a challenge that all rowers experience and for which coaches must plan. Chapter 6 outlined how the organization of training can be optimized to ensure the rower can effectively adapt from both strength and endurance training. However, the appropriate nutritional strategies can support the adaptation process to both endurance training and, more importantly during a concurrent training programme, strength training, where it becomes more difficult to optimize adaptation.

Energy and fluid demands during training

Rowers may experience an exceptionally high volume of training, so fuelling appropriately is essential to withstanding the rigours of training volume and intensity. Male openweight rowers may have energy requirements of 3,500–4,500 kcal per day, with female openweight rower requiring 2,700–3,400 kcal per day. Lightweight male rowers have an energy expenditure of 2,900–3,600 kcal per day, with lightweight females consuming 2,300–2,900 kcal per day. This is clearly a higher energy demand than the normal recommended caloric intake given to sedentary to mildly active individuals. With training, rowers will also increase their fluid loss, which makes hydration critically important too. A slight percentage decrease in hydration can have a marked negative impact on performance, whether endurance or more high intensity efforts. During 90–100 minutes of exercise, male rowers can expect a sweat rate of between 1,200 mL/h in cool conditions to 2,000 mL/h in warmer conditions, with females demonstrating 800 mL/h and 1,400 mL/h in the same conditions.

The main focus of the following sections will be on macronutrients (carbohydrate, fat and protein), specifically carbohydrate and fluid intake. Training nutrition can be broken down to pre-training (preparation to train), during training (sustaining training) and post-training (training recovery). Training nutrition should be viewed as trying to achieve the following three goals:

Refuel (replete glycogen stores)

Rehydrate (replete fluid levels)

Rebuild (cellular adaptation from training augmented with nutrition)

Pre-training nutrition

60–180 minutes before long steady aerobic sessions, it is advisable for the rower to have a carbohydrate meal from a food source with a low glycaemic index (GI). Carbohydrate is broken down into glycogen (a muscle energy source) and absorbed into the muscles through the bloodstream. The rate at which blood glucose levels rise can be measured by the glycaemic index. The higher the index, the more simple the carbohydrate food source (such as cornflakes) and the quicker the rise in blood glucose levels; the lower the index, the more complex the carbohydrate (such as porridge) and the slower the rise in blood glucose levels.

Having a meal with a low GI means the rower is increasing the level of natural glycogen stores within his liver and muscles in preparation for the training session. The low GI carbohydrates have a slow release into the bloodstream and help prevent the glucose dip when training starts. They may also increase fat utilization during steady aerobic training. Examples of low

Nutrition

GI carbohydrates are porridge, muesli, pasta, multi-grain bread and baked beans.

Within an hour of a rowing session high GI foods can be snacked on to improve glycogen stores. By mixing high and low GI carbohydrate foods, a reduction of the glucose dip can be achieved. Most sports drinks have a high GI, as do white bread, bagels and potatoes.

Ensuring hydration is maintained before training is as important as the fuelling. Adequate fluid consumption can be taken from food sources that have high water content or from alternatives to water such as the milk on cereal. Fluid intake should be as much a part of the rower's behaviour as it is a requirement for performance. A rower should be consuming fluid regularly throughout the day and he should be urged to consume fluids with each meal. This should provide enough opportunities for the rower to continually hydrate throughout the day.

The biggest challenge for the rower is the first training session of the day, when club and elite rowers alike will be on the water early in the morning. The challenge is the time between rising from bed and training. Preparation is the key here and again, encouraging behaviours that allow the rower to prepare the food the night before can remove the burden in the morning that may have resulted in occasions where he has not fed pre-training, which is not ideal. Working with a qualified nutritionist will allow for suitable solutions to be found for those who struggle to feed early in the morning.

Within-training nutrition

Within a training session, refuelling allows for the quality of aerobic training to be maintained as the rower replenishes and maintains his glycogen levels. Foods with a higher GI are better utilized during training. Sports drinks and gels provide an effective way to get fuel to the bloodstream. If you are looking for solid food sources within training sessions, bananas, whilst being a medium GI food, are useful as a training snack. In 2014 some new training guidelines came from the Dutch nutritionist Asker Jeukendrup. For a training duration of 30–75 minutes, only small amounts of carbohydrate should be taken; for sessions lasting 1–2 hours, 30g of carbohydrate per hour should be consumed, while 60g per hour is recommended for sessions lasting 2–3 hours.

Maintaining hydration throughout the session will also help to maintain the quality of training by allowing for optimal physiological adaptations. Dehydration can negatively impact not only physiological processes but also cognition. With impaired cognition, the rower will have a reduced ability to understand coaching or crew instruction, and will have an impaired ability to accurately complete skilled tasks such as refining technical components of the rowing stroke. Electrolyte fluids are useful to employ instead of water alone as they are able to maintain hydration without significant consumption of water; the electrolyte content allows for water to be retained more effectively by the body. Thirst rate is not always a good measure of hydration status as, when thirst strikes, the chances are the rower is already dehydrated. Developing behaviours whereby the rower consistently sips on water throughout training is a better strategy. This is easier when training on lakes where there are often short breaks to turn the boat, providing an ideal opportunity to fuel and hydrate. However, on long river training sessions, allowing the rower to hydrate is essential. This becomes an even greater need during the height of summer with high ambient temperatures.

Post-training nutrition

Post-training nutrition has a dual role: ensuring the optimization of training adaptation from the previous session immediately completed, while also preparing the rower for the next training session of the day. It is important that the rower is able to gain as much adaptation from the training session as possible through appropriate nutrition without compromising the next session. Good nutritional behaviours will support both these objectives and do not require different feeding strategies. As highlighted above, refuelling, rehydrating and remodelling are critical post-training. If the above appropriate strategies for pre- and during training have been completed, then the post-training nutrition is a lot easier to complete. However, there are times where post-training nutrition may need to alter as pre- or during training nutrition has been less than optimal, for example due to losing a water bottle in the river or forgetting fuel sources during long outings. If optimal nutrition or hydration strategies are compromised during training for whatever reason, using the post-training nutrition window can be used to rectify this to reduce the impact on the next training session and minimize loss of training adaptation from the previous session.

The body is most responsive to refuelling and rehydrating immediately after training, so it seems logical to use this window (20–30 minutes) to complete both. However, if this is not possible, it will not limit the rate of adaptation or recovery, and this should be seen as a guideline and not a rule. There are compelling arguments suggesting that immune function is compromised for a period of time immediately after exercise, which can be reduced with refuelling and rehydration to bring the immune function back to near-normal levels. To firstly ensure adequate adaptation, the rower needs to ensure he is not in caloric deficit while also replenishing glycogen stores in preparation for the next session. The rower should aim to eat a carbohydrate-rich meal containing both high and low GI foods to support both of these requirements. Consuming 0.8–1.2g of carbohydrate per kg of body mass immediately after training will be sufficient for appropriate recovery and adaptation. For a 76kg female rower, this would be 61–91g of carbohydrate. However, modifications can be made if pre- and during training nutrition has been compromised or a rower is trying to reduce fat mass. These goals should be explored with a qualified nutritionist.

Although rowers have a habit of consuming a carbohydrate-rich meal after long and multiple training sessions during the day, the focus on protein is often overlooked. Protein is the only macronutrient that can stimulate muscle protein synthesis to support muscle strength and hypertrophy (see below section on nutrition for promoting strength adaptation). Protein is also important in aerobic training adaptation. If protein is not adequately consumed, the full potency of a training session will not be met, which may limit mitochondrial biogenesis (production of organelles within a cell that produce the energy for aerobic respiration). Most aerobic training is looking to increase mitochondrial number and function, and protein is required to support this adaptation. As a general rule, consuming 20–25g of protein post-training will be adequate to support biogenesis. This range generally covers the majority of rowers of various body masses. However, 0.3g of protein per kg of body mass will give you a more accurate measure of protein need. Taking the same 76kg female rower mentioned above as an example, this would equate to roughly 23g of protein.

A simple and practical way to maintain hydration is pre- and post-training body mass weighing. While this will give a crude measure of changes in body mass, it can be used to identify how much fluid has potentially been lost during the training session. The rower should attempt to rehydrate himself to his pre-session weight. Consuming 1–1.5 litres per kg of body mass lost is a very loose guideline as everyone is an individual and the

Nutrition

volume depends on the electrolyte content of the fluid. As rowers become more aware of what it takes to rehydrate effectively, individual strategies can be developed to meet their specific rehydration and training needs. The rower should remember to ensure he wears the same clothing pre- and post-training and accounts for sweat loss in training kit or water-soaked kit, as both will impact the accuracy of pre- and post-weighing.

Nutrition for the promotion of strength adaptation

The principles of nutrition (refuel, rehydrate and remodel) do not differ for strength training when compared to aerobic training. However, there is a greater emphasis on muscle fibre adaptation, whether that is increasing its force-producing capability or hypertrophy. While the consumption of carbohydrate and protein content may not actually change when compared to the guidelines above, the rationale is slightly different. Strength training is a potent stimulus of muscle protein synthesis (MPS), although immediately after training there is muscle protein degradation (MPD). Synthesis and degradation occur simultaneously throughout the day but, when one is greater than the other, this is the dominant adaptation. Ensuring MPS is stimulated to a greater degree than MPD is important to optimally repair, rebuild and grow muscle fibres. Protein is also a potent stimulus of MPS so, when combined with strength training, this can increase MPS significantly over MPD. Protein immediately after (and even during) strength training can stimulate more MPS than MPD and actually reduce MPD too, which further optimizes muscle fibre adaptation.

Protein is the only macronutrient that can stimulate MPS, and while carbohydrate can attenuate MPD it cannot stimulate MPS. After a strength training session, MPS can be stimulated up to 48 hours post-exercise. This means that there is a very large window to continually adapt from the strength training session. Following the guidelines on carbohydrate, protein and hydration above will help to continue the adaptation from strength training. As stated, the general rule of 20–25g of protein per serving is very pertinent here. Taking this further, consuming 20–25g of protein (or 0.3g protein per kg of body mass) 4–5 times a day will ensure that MPS is always greater than MPD and keep the rower in a favourable environment to continually adapt and gain the most from the strength training session. Arguments have been made for and against protein consumption during and after strength training. This can be a rower's personal choice as long as the fundamental principles of refuelling, rehydrating and remodelling are followed. By following these principles, protein will always be consumed with carbohydrate and fluids, which will help the rower to optimally adapt and recover.

Race day nutrition

The actual energy cost of rowing a 2,000m race is quite small as the race generally lasts between 5 and 8 minutes depending on boat class, gender, weight category and environmental conditions. Therefore, refuelling and rehydration during the event is not necessary. However, it is important to ensure glycogen stores are fully replenished and the rower is optimally hydrated to ensure there is immediate energy for the rower throughout the event and dehydration does not impact cognitive decision-making or technical competency. The biggest energy costs of race day performance are the warm-ups and paddles or ergometer work that may be completed throughout the day. Using the pre-, during and post-training guidelines will satisfactorily meet the energy and hydration demands of race day.

Nutrition

Often race nerves mean a rower loses appetite and eats less. It is important to have a race day food plan and that the rower has had some input and control over what he will consume to fuel and recover with. Generally, simple and plain food is better digested and absorbed. Rehearsing the race day nutrition strategy is also advised, so that the rower knows what to expect. This becomes more important for those who have less racing history.

Race day nutrition is especially important at a multi-day event because it is quite difficult for the rower to maintain a stable weight with irregular meal times and loss of appetite. Sports drinks, gels and replacement meals are all useful ways to keep the rower refuelled and at a stable body weight at a regatta. Following the previous guidelines around refuelling, rehydrating and to a lesser extent remodelling, a rower will not go too far wrong in organizing his race day regatta nutrition strategy.

Supplementation

Nutritional supplements have grown in popularity within and outside the sporting population. They are often heavily advertised and spoken about within the media and sporting circles, often with claims of improvement in performance and physiology that are backed with pseudo-science. Rowers should not use nutritional supplements in an arbitrary manner; the biggest performance, health and physiology gains will come from good nutritional practices.

Nutritional supplements have been the cause of many inadvertent doping positive tests and potentially can cause ill health. It is the intention here to inform the reader what due processes should be completed prior to rowers considering using supplements.

However, before discussing this further, it is important to note that from 1 January 2015, the World Anti-Doping Agency (WADA) updated code came into effect, with Athlete Support Personnel (ASP) being included under the anti-doping jurisdiction of WADA. ASPs can be anyone who supports a rower in preparation for training or competition, including the coach and support staff. Therefore, if advice is given around supplementation that leads to a rower's positive test, that person is equally culpable under the WADA code, which can lead to bans on working with athlete populations. The WADA website is a great resource for finding out what the rules and violations are and how to support rowers to make correctly informed choices around what they decide to use (https://www.wada-ama.org/). For those in the UK, Informed Sport is a company that tests supplements for banned substances. Informed Sport lists a number of products that have gone through its certification process and are deemed to be free of these substances. While this gives the consumer an added layer of knowledge of the quality of the product, all should be aware that this still does not give any athlete protection against supplements that may be contaminated. More details on Informed Sport can be found at http://informed-sport.com/.

Rowers and support staff, including coaches, need to make informed choices around what supplementations are worth investing in. There is always an inherent risk in using them, even if it is very small. For those in the UK, USA and Canada, Global Drug Reference Online (http://www.globaldro.com/) is a resource with information about the prohibited status of specific medications based on the current WADA prohibited list. This is an exceptional tool for athletes and support personnel alike to protect athletes from prohibited medications.

Secondly, the use of supplementation is not a shortcut to performance improvements or sudden increases in training performance. There is no substitute for training effectively with the end goal in mind. Supplementation

Nutrition

should be an aid to improving training adaptation or assisting in performance. However, before embarking on the use of supplementation, rowers should attempt to train and compete without it to determine the actual physiological performance of which the rower is capable. If the use of supplementation is being considered, rowers and coaches should initially have appropriate medical health checks and a discussion with a doctor before taking any supplementation to ensure the rower is not likely to increase any risk to his health. Invest in getting appropriate advice from reputable nutritional or physiology practitioners who understand the impact of what is safe and effective while also discussing the real benefit of using them over food and good training.

For instance, supplementing with carbohydrate gels during long training outings is no substitute for being able to fuel such outings with the energy stores the body has already. Supplementation may reduce the body's own ability to supply the energy requirements effectively, or blunt the training adaptation. If fat utilization is a key training goal to help a rower reduce total body fat, the use of carbohydrate gels will increase blood sugar levels and become the primary energy source. This is just one example of how misuse of supplementation can affect training outcomes.

For the UK, the Sport and Exercise Nutrition Register (www.senr.org.uk) has been set up to give consumers confidence in nutrition practitioners by accrediting those who have completed the rigorous competency-based assessment, which a number of organizations do not use. This is a new and ever-expanding organization where appropriate nutritionists can be found.

A final note on supplementation: there are many products currently available to rowers and other athletes alike. Some of the claims made for the performance benefits they offer may not be true as they are not supported by scientific rigour, or if they are capable of huge performance gains they may not be legal. It cannot be stressed enough that the responsibility lies solely with the rower as to what he consumes, and the coach and support staff have a responsibility to help facilitate excellent behaviours around nutrition and supplementation. Supplementation may only provide small training or performance gains, whereas good organization of effective training and excellent nutritional habits will give significantly larger gains to the rower.

CHAPTER 12

MENTAL SKILLS

The mind needs the same attention in training as the body does for a rower to reach his potential. A rower needs to learn how to train, recover, row, race and win. This happens in the early morning and late afternoons of training on the water and in the gym, on the cold days away from the regatta venue.

No rower is ever the 'full package' and all have to work hard at building upon their strengths and reducing their weaknesses. The rower needs to have a plan and an understanding of himself. Confidence is a key ingredient to any performance.

Confidence

Confidence is the rower's belief that his performance will be there on race day for him to deliver. Confidence needs to be built on evidence through training. What can he do better than the opposition? What parameter is he aiming to achieve that he has never done before? To answer these questions the rower has to have his self-belief and confidence developed through his training.

He has to be challenged and he may well fail. If he does, he will need to build himself back up stronger, physically and mentally. The training environment and regime need to have constructive competition and a learning environment to challenge and develop the rower in this way.

A rower needs to know his strengths and work hard to them: that is the best place to start building and developing confidence. Acknowledging and understanding his strengths allows him to keep on delivering them and be less concerned about any negativity or confidence zappers surrounding his weakness.

How he displays and presents his body language and his self-talk can affect his confidence both positively and negatively. He needs to have a mixture of being positive, realistic and honest. He should be looking to develop a deep and robust confidence. Confidence is not about papering over cracks – it's about identifying and addressing what needs to be done and working hard, exploiting strengths to get there.

A rower should use a training diary to reflect and record his training. This is also a tool to record the evidence that lays the foundation for his confidence. Using a few pages to record what has been done session by session can build confidence and prepare for times and situations that will be challenging and potentially reduce confidence.

Setting and achieving goals are also fundamental to building confidence.

Goal setting

Whether a rower's aim is to live a healthy and active life or to pursue an Olympic dream, he needs goals. There are two types of goals: outcome and process.

The outcome goal is what you get when you put all the processes together. An outcome goal might be completing a 6:00 minute 2,000m performance on the ergometer at race cadence.

Mental Skills

The process goals are the ones that build up to that performance. In this example, the rower will need to have the power, endurance and technical competence to hold a 1:30 split for 6 minutes. Process goals may well be achieving:

- Progressive training targets, for example, 500m at 1:30 pace, 1,000m at 1:30 pace, 1,500m at 1:30 pace.
- Maintaining rowing length when the stroke rate increases by increasing power with the legs and hips and moving the hands away quicker from the finish.
- Maintaining drive and recovery sequences at race pace: legs, trunk and arms for the drive; arms, trunk and legs for the recovery.
- Progressive strength and conditioning targets so that the rower is strong enough to do the programme required, holds technical form and also has the conditioning to hold technical form for the whole 2,000m.

Another way to do it is to have:

- 'Why' goals – outcome and big picture.
- 'What' goals – the key impact and performance indicators that are required to achieve the Why goals.
- 'How' goals – the attitudes, practices and techniques done on a daily basis that will achieve the What goals.

Ergometer performance is an interesting beast. In international side-by-side water races where the rower faces backwards and has to sprint out from the start to fight for an advantage and control the race, he goes into oxygen debt and accumulates lactic acid that can only be repaid once the race is over. The 2,000m ergometer test is no less brutal, but the nature of man versus machine means that a more efficient racing tactic can be employed and the rower should aim for a more even strategy if he wants to maximize his score. The feedback on commercially available machines is very reliable and they are good tools for exploring pacing strategy. With that feedback every stroke, the rower can work to the average split of his target score and be in good enough physical shape to attack the second half of the ergometer race.

A rower's pacing is developed through his training. Goal setting and prioritizing within his training programme and sessions will allow him to practise and 'feel' for the rhythm and pace that he will need in racing. The more often he can replicate this in training, the more predictable it will be in racing.

Visualization

Visualization and imagery are important skills for a rower to develop. What you see is what you get. Visualization creates a greater understanding in the rower of what he can see of himself, his technique and his performance. Through visualization the rower can create and recreate his perfect stroke, his perfect rhythm, his perfect race.

Visualization can be created using all the body's senses: the feel of the run of the hull in the water, the sense of synchronicity and rhythm of the crew, the sound of the blade entry into the water, the sight of the person in front in perfect time.

Having a clear technical picture of what his

TIPS FOR THE ROWER WHEN GOAL SETTING AND ACHIEVING:

- Set realistic outcome and process goals.
- Make sure they don't sit in the drawer – have a sense of urgency.
- Record your progress.
- Regularly review.

stroke should look and feel like can also get the rower playing back and imagining his perfect stroke while he is away from the boat. This will help him move to that technical image.

Visualization of race plans and race rehearsal are also popular. A cox or coach can call the race strategy and plan while the crew visualizes the race, honing in on the cox's calls and feeling or rehearsing the crew's race strategy so that on race day the crew can present itself on the same page and be ready to deliver to its potential. Similar race rehearsal can be done while the crew is rowing.

Being relaxed is a prerequisite to quality visualization. It may be enough for the rower to have some quiet sitting time concentrating on rhythmic breathing, or one of the many other relaxation, yoga and centering techniques may provide a better platform for relaxation control.

Reviewing

Reviewing, briefing and debriefing both training and racing allow the rower to have a more in-depth understanding of his performance and training, as well as setting priorities on where he needs to place his focus next.

Simply put, the rower needs no more than three things to go out and implement during a training session or race (most of the time it should just be one). At the end of the session or race these points need to be assessed and priorities set and agreed for the next outing. This process adds clarity and helps identify the priority issues that the crew can change.

A greater understanding of how the rower's performance is achieved makes him able to repeat it more often and become consistent with his success. Using his training diary, the rower can record these points and build his confidence from how the crew and his rowing develop. As the rower and crew develop these skills they should be previewing their performance and predicting what it will be.

The key to good reviewing is asking the right questions and the crew being able to communicate honestly, directly and sometimes robustly.

Race routines

Pre-race routines start at race time and work back. Rowers – what do you want to be thinking on the start line? What do you want to be thinking 2, 5, 30 minutes or an hour before the start? Do you get nervous, too nervous? Not nervous enough? What should you be thinking? Being ready to race and deliver your best is obviously crucial to everyone that races either on the water or ergometer. The more consistent the pre-race routines, the more predictable a rower's performance tends to be.

Being able to choose what mental state and emotion to display can be an innate thing but can also be learnt. The first step is being able to recognize which emotion and mind state you are in at the start or in the race. What is the difference between anxious and fearful or determined and aggressive? Having recognized the subtleties between emotions, you can consider what the different feelings and physical characteristics are and how they either enhance or impede the delivery of your performance. Having ascertained what works best for you, that mindset and emotion can be practised and awareness of it increased in training and racing.

It's also important that the period before the race allows a rower to be in physical and technical form when he arrives at the start.

The race warm-up needs to be practised so that the rower and his crew know what to expect on race day. A light run, bike or ergometer and stretch on land before boating allows for a general warm-up before heading out on the water. The length of time that these need to take varies with individuals. On the water the rower and crew need to have enough time

Mental Skills

to technically come together and do enough pieces to be confident that they have done enough good strokes in the warm-up to bring into the race.

> **TOP TIPS FOR ROWERS AND CREWS ON RACE DAY**
>
> - Plan your race day – allow more time than you need so you don't need to rush.
> - Let the day unfold.
> - Manage your emotions.
> - The on-water warm-up should raise your base body temperature.
> - Make sure you have done a long piece to be in race rhythm in the race direction during the warm-up.
> - Do a racing start in the race direction.

CHAPTER 13

CONCLUSION

We hope that you have seen the rationale of building training by understanding the key components of a rowing performance and the physiological, psychological and technical parameters that underpin that performance.

Training priorities will be set relating to the rower's training age and experience, and the programme will need to constantly challenge and adapt in order for the rower's physiological adaptation to be optimized.

Rowing technique and excellence should be pursued as an integral part of the rower's programme, with specific training as well as exercises on land and water that will enhance and develop his technical ability.

Balance and variety in training is important, as is monitoring and testing the rower to ascertain his performance and training development.

Mobility, resistance and strength training are important components of training to build a rower's robustness, muscle mass and specific rowing strength. Like rowing technique, it is important to spend time learning how to develop strength exercise technique.

Accompanying training, nutrition and recovery play a key role in a rower's adaptation to training stimulus and should not be overlooked.

Training the body without training the mind to get the most out of the rower's capacity will leave him short of reaching his potential. Embedding mental skills and challenges into a rower's training environment and programme makes for a vibrant, focused regime.

INDEX

2,000m ergometer 48–51

adolescent strength training 70–73
aerobic pathway 10
aerobic training 38–40
agility 53
alactic system 10
anaerobic pathway 10
anaerobic training 41, 47

back squat 96–98
bench press 100–102
bench pull 102–103

coaching 44
circulatory system 11
circuit training 52, 54–55
concurrent training 69–70, 115
confidence 121
core stability 105, 106, 107–108
coxswain training 112–113
cross training 18

deadlift 98–100

energy systems 10–11
ergometer competitions 48–51
ergometer training sessions 47–48

flexibility 81, 88–90
fluid demands 115

gearing and rigging 41–44
goal setting 121–122

intent 73

lactate tolerance training 47
leverage 19

mobility 81–82
  ankle 82–83
  hip 83–85
  spine 85–86
muscularity 11

nutrition supplements 119–120

oxygen consumption 9

post training nutrition 116–118
power clean 91–96
pre training nutrition 115

race day nutrition 118–119
race routines 123–124
respiratory system 11
rowing stroke
  catch 25
  common faults 28–30
  drive phase 20–21
  early recovery 27
  early drive 25
  finish and release 26
  grip 23
  late drive 26
  late recovery 28
  mid drive 25
  mid recovery 27

Index

placement 24
posture 22
recovery phase 22
seat position 22

sample rowing training sessions 38–41
strength conditioning training 64–66
strength training 56–58
   explosive strength testing 79
   explosive strength training 61–62
   for the developing rower 70–73
   functional strength training 73–75
   heavy strength testing 78–79
   heavy strength training 58–61
   hypertrophy testing 62–64
   hypertrophy training 79–80
   nutrition 118
   philosophy 57
stroke correction 30–37

training adaptation 16–17
training aids 45
training priorities 13–15
training programme development 12
trunk 104, 106
   trunk Endurance 108–109
   trunk Strength 111–112

visualisation 122–123
VO2 max 12

weightlifting technique 68–69
within training nutrition 116

RELATED TITLES FROM CROWOOD

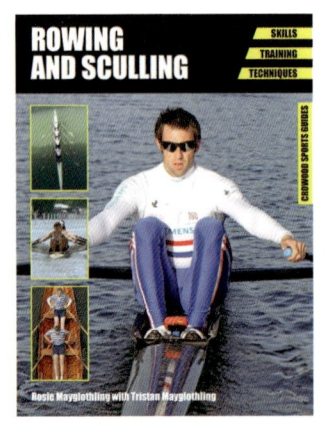

Crowood Sports Guide: Rowing and Sculling
978 1 84797 746 5

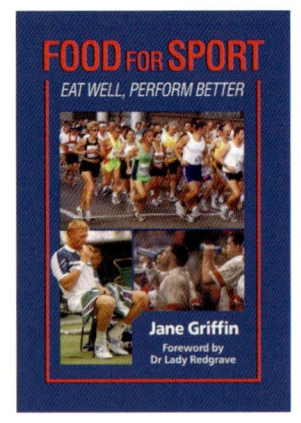

Food for Sport
978 1 86126 216 5

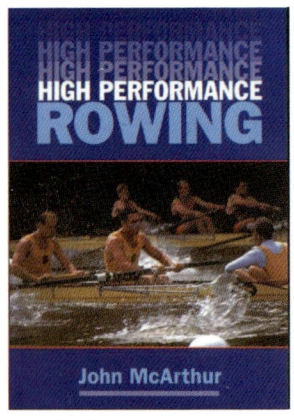

High Performance Rowing
978 1 86126 039 0

Sculling
978 1 86126 758 0

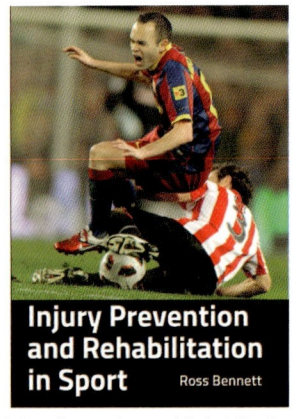

Injury Prevention and Rehabilitation for Sport
978 1 84797 957 5

Principles and Practice of Weight Training
978 1 84797 488 4

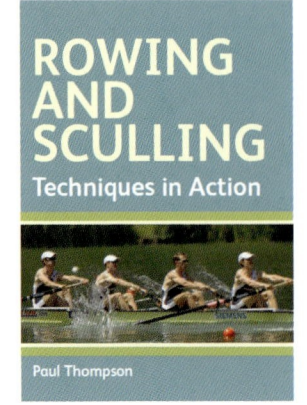

Rowing and Sculling DVD
978 1 84797 006 0

In case of difficulty ordering, please contact the Sales Office:
The Crowood Press
Ramsbury
Wiltshire
SN8 2HR
UK

Tel: 44 (0) 1672 520320

enquiries@crowood.com

www.crowood.com